Advance Praise for...

Customer Service and Beyond...
It is All About the WOW!

"What a great read! I've seen this author in a training environment and am confident this book will supplement the concepts she discusses. I intend to purchase copies for several of my clients."

Holli Martin, President
Hype Creative

"A must-have for teaching customer service excellence. This easy-to-read text applies principles and concepts by entertaining descriptions of actual occurrences—applicable to any business or service entity."

Patricia Peverly,
Chief Nursing Officer
Anderson Hospital

"Dawn Mushill consistently receives outstanding evaluations when providing either customer service workshops or a keynote speech. Dawn's high marks are due to two attributes; a **passion** for WOW customer service and a **personality** that is entertaining yet professional. These attributes jump off every page of this must-read book."

Sally Koval,
Center for Workforce Training

"As I read through the chapters, I was touched by the stories of ordinary people doing extraordinary customer service (or missing the chance); I kept thinking of people in my life who needed to hear this story or that. My Christmas shopping is already done; I'm treating friends and coworkers to this wonderful guide to service excellence."

Larry Bear, Administrator
Jersey Community Hospital

"Dawn has given us the *Bridget Jones* of customer service, blending humor and humanity through anecdote and example. And in the process, sneaky person that she is, she trains and teaches, reminding us of all the misplaced dos and don'ts of the service industry. Thanks, Dawn. Crank up the bass...and keep singing."

Jenna Garrett
Writer and Copyeditor
~ WordWorks

"I loved it! Refreshing and right on...couldn't put it down! Your personal stories, with the humorous way that you related them, are a keen insight for all...particularly those of us in the hospitality industry. It will be a 'must-read' for my employees at the Tourism Bureau Southwestern Illinois."

Jo Kathmann, President/CEO
Tourism Bureau Southwestern
Illinois

"Dawn's approach to customer service is simple and to the point. This book will help you to clearly understand from the customer's point of view as to what they want, and from the business point of view on how to deliver optimum service."

Dennis Chandler, Owner
Pizza Man
~ Troy, IL

"As a manager of a regional-based company, I found that this publication provided me with the tools to better serve my clients."

Lisa Zabawa
Troy Branch Manager
~ Assistant Vice President
First National Bank of Staunton

"Dawn has a very down to earth and realistic approach on how to improve customer service and create that 'WOW' experience. Reading this book filled with her life experiences puts into perspective how very simple good customer service could be and how very lacking it is today."

Katie Hopkins,
Executive Vice President
Truck Centers, Inc.

Dawn Mushill – what a great teacher, mentor, motivator, and now author!

I am excited to see this book jump to life with its comic relief, while at the same time teaching the importance of being in the moment—not only in the business sector of customer service, but in our personal lives as well. I have been fortunate to experience Dawn's energy for life and business in person on many occasions, and I am always amazed as she continues to do it with confidence, dignity, and professionalism—always willing to offer up that helping hand.

Thanks for adding another helpful tool to my culinary repertoire.

Renèe Robertson,
Owner & Executive Chef
Renèe's Gourmet Catering, Inc.
~ Collinsville, IL

"A must read for anyone who wants to improve their people skills! I would recommend this book to my friends in the service industry, as well as to individuals who want to enhance the way they communicate and interact with others."

Marietta Miller
Illinois Federation of Teachers

"Dawn Mushill teaches us that Customer Service is not something we put on and take off as we enter and leave the workforce each day. To excel at Customer Service, Dawn, in her unique and enthusiastic manner, reveals how others perceive us and inspires us to improve our lives above and beyond the workforce."

> Harry Hutchison, President
> National Bank
> ~ Hillsboro, IL

"Thanks for letting me read the preview of your book. It is light and easy to read. I love the actual experiences you reference! I can picture myself in those situations...especially the *be in the moment.* This is so true...I find myself not being in the moment with my children more than in my professional role; however, it is so TRUE!!"

> Joell Aguirre
> River Bend Growth Association
> ~ Godfrey, IL

"How very like Dawn to take life's experiences and turn them into lessons in a book."

> Jean Myers
> Madison County Board Member

"Dawn's book is a must-read for anyone wanting to take their service level to another step."

> Mayor Tom Caraker
> Troy, IL

Customer Service and Beyond

...It is all about the WOW!

Stellar strategies to WOW your customers!

Dawn Mushill

Femme Osage Publishing
St. Louis, Missouri
2008

First Edition

ISBN: 978-1-934509-22-7

Library of Congress Control Number: 2008936218

Printed in the United States of America.

First printing: 2008

Cover illustration by:
       Cyanotype.ca

Published by:
       Femme Osage Publishing
       1301 Colby Drive
       Saint Peters, Missouri 63376
       FemmeOsagePublishing.com

Table of Contents

Foreword

    I have long had a dream to offer the public a book to help pilot them in the customer service industry, and in doing so—whether by accident or design—create a cheat sheet for myself that would serve as both a refresher course and support for whatever it was or wasn't that went well or badly during any given day. Those moments happen...to all of us.

    I have always felt that many people go into the service arena, often as a first job, totally unprepared and unarmored for the challenges ahead of them. We have all had experiences that are less than pleasant, and in some instances intolerable, at the hands of people serving us—people who, either from lack of knowledge, heavy workload or unfortunately from indifference, have turned us, as customers, to other venues to spend our money. The result? Loss of profits, perhaps even failure, for those businesses.

    This book is not intended for one specific rung of the employment ladder. It applies to upper management as fully as it does to new trainees and every level in between, exhibiting those things to do and those not to do, good behavior and inadequate behavior, and aspects of successful businesses versus those that will likely fail. My hope is that all of you profit in some way from the information, by making your particular job or business a thriving, dynamic, and more rewarding entity.

August, 2008

From the Author

When I ultimately committed to the challenge of writing this book, I knew there would be a wealth of long, late, solitary hours at the keyboard; and yet that I didn't get here alone. Not at all. As any of you would have done, I rehashed and drew upon past experiences, the environment I'd been brought up in, people of memorable influence and assistance whether *because of* or *in spite of*, and those who either directly or indirectly contributed to who I was and who I've become. To those people I offer a sincere *thank you*.

For many years I have written for, taught, and presented seminars on the subject of the service industry, hopefully lending further credibility to my lifelong association with that area of work. My parents, George and Sue Johnson, worked for their entire adult lives serving others. My mother owns and operates her own business and has worked in the service industry for more than 40 years. She has taught me many things, as moms have a way of doing—and among the high-ranking lessons is that any and all customers deserve to be treated with dignity even though it's not always a recip-rocal process. My late father was a musician, and in the working world it was so easy to see that his first concern was the customer. There were undoubtedly many times when he would have preferred to please himself in the choice of what he played, but he was smart and caring enough to know that the best way to get customers back on a steady basis was to please *them*. Between the two of them they taught me, as I would encourage you, to pursue any laudable goal regardless of how difficult achieving it might be—that all things are possible to someone who works hard and puts forth the necessary effort to attain that goal. For what I learned from my parents, for what I continue to learn because of them, I am truly thankful.

To my husband Ted, who has supported me throughout this entire process, thank you for allowing me to follow my dream and handing me the map when I needed it.

Dawn

Dedication

This book is dedicated to all of those who wish to raise the
bar of customer service,
and then raise it again...and again...
and to my father and mother
who were the first to teach me how.

Acknowledgements

I need to thank those people who have believed in and supported enough of my "crazy" ideas to help get me to where I am today. It's a good place to be. It would have been easy for me to quit on a few things along the way, but I'm glad I didn't. Thanks for your strength, your wisdom, and your patience—and that sturdy nudge now and then.

My husband, Ted Mushill, who sat alone through too many meals while I attended undergraduate and graduate school and worked on this book. He has always been supportive of my career and has always encouraged me to do whatever makes me happy.

My Mom and Dad, George and Sue Johnson, who taught me customer service through their role as *customer servers*. As parents they were the ultimate educators, tossing in a good mix of believing in myself, that anything is possible, that everything happens for a reason, and that music is a magical and important piece of life.

My sister, Terri Johnson, who has inspired me by her entrepreneurship. She owns her own business and is a great Mom, but then she learned from a pro. She shows me that it is important to enjoy life and that planning things ahead is not always the best way. (Did I just say that?)

My niece, Bailey Johnson, who has taught me to live in the moment and inspires me to try new things. She is apparently destined to carry on my obsessive compulsive legacy, and reminds me daily of how I drove everyone crazy while I was growing up. It's her turn now.

My Mother-in-Law, Pat Mushill, for showing me support and that there are more meals to cook than tuna casserole.

My mentor, boss, and friend, Kris Gamm-Smith, who taught me how to be a good leader and that there is something good in every person.

My mentor, Judi Sparks, who gave me my first opportunity to teach, and who has always been one of my biggest supporters.

My buddy, Jeff Maclin, for saying in my first interview with the Troy/Maryville Area Chamber of Commerce, "I want to hear more from this girl. She has passion."

My Grandma Liz Stevens and my Grandma Alice Hill, for teaching me kindness and the importance of thank-you cards.

My friend, Holli Martin, who has shown me the endless possibilities of going out on your own!

My neighbor, Jean Draves, for helping me discover my love of reading by taking me to the library every Saturday morning.

My Chamber of Commerce Presidents, Gerry Eckert, Jeff Maclin, Linda Manley, Jean Myers, Mike Johnson, and Lisa Zabawa, for leading by example and also allowing me to take risks in moving the Chamber forward.

My friend, Bonnie Levo, for helping me through one of the most difficult times of my life. You will never know how much your help meant to me.

My grandparents, Wanda & Dwight Cook and Walter & Alta Johnson, who showed me love and support my entire life and taught me that being the first grandchild on both sides was a great thing!

My friend, Joyce Virgin, who always has kind words and a smiling face to make my day.

My friend, Denise Cook, for her constant encouragement and support of everything I have ever pursued.

My three favorite teachers, Mr. George Amisch, Mr. Ed Bodnam and Ms. Patricia Dineff, for pushing me hard to study and teaching me that I had it in me.

My boss and friend, Sarah Allen, who is the epitome of professionalism.

My friend and Scrabble partner, Judi Burnside, who taught me how important it is to have a little fun in life and the sheer magnitude of keeping her away from the triple word score!

My friend, Bill Mahoney, for believing in me early in my career.

My boss and friend, Sally Koval, for taking a chance on me as a trainer and supporting me throughout.

My friend, Mayor Tom Caraker, for believing in me and encouraging me to pursue my dreams.

My friends, Bill and Gwen Berutti, for their support of my family and allowing my Dad to live his dream.

My friend, George Rafeedie, who was always there for me at CCC, and is one of my biggest fans.

My confidante, Nancy Bracey (LCPC), for her confidence in me and her help in taking my life to another level. She has inspired me to be someone that I have always wanted to be, and I will be forever indebted to her for her help and support.

My friend, Bill Clark, for his support of me and his love for our family.

My editor, Gloria Horrell, who encouraged me when I had almost given up on the book. Thank you, Gloria. This book has become a reality because of you.

My extended family, for encouraging me through school, through my career, and through life. All of you have helped to make me who I am today.

Introduction

"One of the deep secrets of life
is that all that is really worth the doing
is what we do for others."
~ Lewis Carroll ~

...or so said the man who wrote *Alice's Adventures in Wonderland*. And whether he was weaving a nonsense fantasy for children or validating what we've all felt in the appreciation and accomplishment of doing for others, Carroll was classically correct. The leap from personal giving to business and occupational service isn't that much of a stretch; and the same rules and repercussions apply. Still, not everyone is designed to work in the service industry—agreed? Unfortunately for us, *and* often for them, many choose that career field anyway...or the career chooses *them* through simple logistics and availability. In many cases a person's entry into the workforce—that coveted first job—is a service-industry one, where they receive little or no training and yet become that all-important first impression the company presents to its customers. Falling down the rabbit hole was nothing compared to the misfortunes that can arise in the real world, and what this means to the company's bottom line is ultimately lost profit, often gathering further casualties along the way in the guise of lost customers and lost employees.

People say that service is "not like it used to be." Personally, and maybe I am just too young, I have no recall of receiving *consistently* excellent service. Sure, there was the corner market where everyone knew you or the local gas station where you knew the attendant (and he actually pumped your gas). But, overall, my memories of service are what they are today—very rarely excellent. What is it that makes service excellent? By simplest definition, it is when the customer leaves satisfied beyond his expectations—and then returns. Yes, even for the large businesses it can make a differ-ence...and this book takes a look at service from every angle, often finding the good and the bad (and the rarely great).

While there are sections for businesses, staff, managers, and customers, you may easily find yourself overlapping into multiple categories—but that's as it should be. My recom-mendation is that you read the entire book to understand the philosophy, as all elements are interrelated; problems and fixes are dependent on a number of variables, some huge, some tiny. I've met people who have gone the extra mile. I have also met people who not only don't go an extra *inch* but launch a service tug-of-war guaranteed to have no winners. I know you know those people. It is easy for us to recognize the person who failed to wait on us properly or failed to say "thank you," but I think it is equally as important to turn the mirror, to look deep inside to make sure we are giving the service that we ourselves expect. I know you have heard the phrase "do onto others"; but when it comes to customer service I am not certain that we always do just that. Everyone stumbles on occasion, but thank goodness there's usually a save.

And because of that this book offers tools as well as safety nets. I want to assist you in making the customer's experience an excellent one that has them saying, "I want to go back." There are so many things that come into play with a customer's encounter—body language, eye contact, first impressions, the handshake, surroundings—and so much of it is overlooked. Small details often seem unimportant when you're focused on the big picture. I hope to open people's eyes to what they are missing—no matter how small.

It's interesting to know that those of you reading this book actually comprise the top 25% in the customer service field. Good for you! Those in the bottom 25% apparently don't know what customer service *is* so they wouldn't even think to be turning these pages. The simple fact that you are reading these words guarantees that we aren't starting from scratch.

But poor Alice...if there had been a greeter, an information desk or even a handy you-are-here mall map in Wonderland, I know she would have gotten home a lot sooner.

Chapter One

Confessions of a Secret Shopper

"Confession is good for the sale."
~ Corey Ford ~

Not for even the briefest childhood moment did I ever once consider a grownup life of intrigue and undercover work. So then just who *is* that moving stealthily past the produce... dipping into a crouch as she peers over the melons...darting furtive glances over her shoulder as she ambles the aisle at the discount store, quietly humming the *Mission Impossible* theme as she whispers into her cell phone? I'm not really certain, but you might want to give her plenty of space. There's one thing guaranteed: it's not a secret shopper.

I guess I should say at least it's not *me*...unless I'm having a serious out-of-body experience that results in zero recall. When I'm in secret shopper mode I lean more toward the invisible, blending in with whatever consumer group it is that I'm currently posing as a part of. I'm just another customer—another shopper, another potential client checking on loan rates, another "uninformed" female asking about oil changes.

When people learn about the *benefits* of being a secret shopper, it's small wonder that most of them envy the job. I mean, who wouldn't? The perks can be wonderful as you often get complimentary meals, enjoy gratis hotel stays, get free oil changes, and receive any number of smaller tokens of appreciation that allow you to do, or thank you for doing, the job. All of this in return for just a little bit of your time...or so it would appear on the surface. But trust me when I say that there is more to secret shopping than meets the eye.

While secret shopping and the report it generates are rarely the first and last maneuvers in company assistance, the best and most long lasting results come from the normal full-service progression—with secret shopping being step one of the support I provide. Companies often initially contact me for training; but in order to develop the individualized guidance requested, secret shopping is necessary to determine all the areas in need of help.

My clients often ask that I secret shop their location(s), during which time I take (mostly mental) note of every aspect of the business. Primary focus often targets service, cleanliness, staff actions and *reactions*—but nothing, large or small, goes unobserved. In every instance I'm able to find things that management has overlooked; and I can't count the number of managers who have told me, "I walk by that every single day, and I've never really seen it." It always comes as a surprise to them, but it is the simplest of concepts. Viewing a business through customer perception, allowing a fresh pair of eyes and ears to see, hear, and experience the everyday norm, produces *very* interesting discoveries. And following that, I highlight and detail their organization's strengths and weaknesses as I compile the report—which allows me to develop a training program that will take the staff, and the company as a whole, to the next level of excellence.

What do I find when I secret shop? Oh, you can only imagine. I have interrupted staff while they were reading their magazine, eating their lunch, doing their hair, painting their nails, plucking their eyebrows, and even putting on deodorant. I have seen more cleavage than I care to ever see again. If you flip it over—literally—I have seen more thong underwear and tattoos on the backside to allow me any degree of professional comfort level with the strangers who are flaunting them. It's an enlightening job.

I have overheard staff bashing their management and management bashing their staff; experienced rude personnel, unclean toilets, poor signage, outdated flyers, overflowing trashcans and bulletin boards—it is endless. But all has not been bad. I have also received service that has literally knocked my socks off (and it takes a lot to do that). Sometimes the service was so good that I felt guilty for not purchasing more. These people clearly "got it". The entire experience was flawless, from the time I walked in to the time I left and all of the time in between.

And there are also those *special* moments when "the shopper" becomes so ingrained that I find myself secret shopping even when I am not supposed to be. This can be, among other things, very confusing to my husband. There have been times when we've gone out to dinner, been sitting at the table waiting for our meal, when he'd lean toward me and whisper, "Do I have to go to the restroom?" I don't know—do you? When we are secret shopping there are obviously places where I'm not allowed; so it's up to Ted and his checklist of things to look for in the men's restroom to fill in some of those blanks.

I often wonder if I wore a hat that said "secret shopper," what would they do differently? And why should it come to that? My goal is to train the staff to treat everyone equal, every single time, secret shopper or not—to steer the company in the direction of excellent customer service.

Service—At All Levels

One day I pulled into the gas pumps at a convenience store. I had just received my new debit card for that gas station and I placed it into the slot. For whatever reason, the card did not work so I tried it again. It did not work—again. So, I slid it in for the third time. As I was pulling out the card I heard this booming voice say, "Push ... the ... card ... in ... sloooooooowly." What? Was *God* talking to me?

As I looked around, I noticed the two clerks inside laughing at me. So, I pulled out my card and went inside. I walked through the door looking right at them, but both were too embarrassed to look me in the eye. I went over to the soda fountain, filled my cup and approached the counter. The person who had spoken to me over the speaker was standing at the register next to the one who waited on me. I set my soda down and said, "Don't worry about how you treated me. And there's no need to bother explaining it to your boss. You see, I am a secret shopper for your company and it's all been documented. I'll have everything in the report." Smiling now, "Have a great evening."

I am going to tell you right now that there is no doubt in my mind that both boys wet their pants! You see, the company they work for holds all employees accountable for each and every secret shopping report. I frequent that store quite often but never saw those two young men again. My bet is that they left before they had the chance of getting fired.

"Sarcasm is just one more service we offer."
~ Anonymous ~

When Business Gets Tough, the Tough Go Shopping

I have worked as a secret shopper for many companies. The basic process of posing as a customer, making detailed observations of problems and service issues, and then completing a report of recommendations for the owners or management requires that I be completely discreet—mostly keeping track of the information mentally, with very little note taking, if any.

Often times I go to lunch by myself afterward, so that I can get my thoughts together. I will make notes for that day, and it helps me get everything out of my head. As I'm doing this, so many people at the restaurant think that I am secret shopping *them*. I often see waitresses running to their boss and pointing me out. Once they do that, I can always count on the manager stepping to my table to ask if everything is okay. What the manager *doesn't* realize is that by doing this he has made it completely obvious, since he didn't stop at tables other than mine.

My point of this story is this – what would you do differently for your customers if you thought each and every one of them were a secret shopper? What if the outcome of your secret shopping report affected your salary? It's just one more reason why we should treat everyone the best and never have to worry about seeking out those we think are secret shoppers.

If your company has never heard of secret shoppers, they should consider the advantages and feedback that they can provide. It is amazing what types of companies can be secret shopped. For example, when I acquired a very large contract with local hospitals, people said "how can you secret shop a hospital?" Actually, it was one of the easiest clients. Think about it. You are in a hospital, and the staff is so busy and involved (or at least they should be) that basically no one is paying attention to you. Other companies to secret shop for include financial institutions, restaurants, legal offices, medical facilities, schools, churches—the list is endless.

Often I am asked to competitive secret shop, which means that I secret shop a few of a company's competitors, make notes, and take them back to my client. We find out what their competitors are selling, what they are upselling, their service, etc. and go from there. There is a lot that you can learn from your competitor. Remember, in order to be the best in your business, you have to be better than your best competitor.

Let's say you have worked somewhere for two years. What is the likelihood of your noticing a mark on the wall or a stain in the carpet? Probably not much, since you are in the same environment every day. It is often recommended to obtain an outsider's point of view, and that can come from many sources. One of the easiest may be comment cards from customers. Have them easily accessible to the customer and pay attention to their suggestions. Another method is to hire someone to act as an observer, who will follow up with a report; still another is to simply enter your facility from a different direction and do your best to look at the environment from an outside point of view.

What could you learn about your company from a secret shopper? A lot. What could you learn by *being* one for your competitors? Maybe even more.

Notes to Employees

I was in line, waiting for service, and noticed the following handwritten sign in all caps:

"THE SECRET SHOPPER IS SUPPOSED TO BE HERE THIS WEEK.

IF YOU DON'T DO GOOD, THEN YOU ARE GONE."

Wow. I have to tell you that the manager responsible for posting that sign is no longer employed with the company.

How motivating is the sign? Instead of posting that sign, why not go over a checklist with your employees of the expectations for *all* customers. Then it will not matter who the secret shopper is or when they come in. Otherwise, when it *is* necessary to post signs for your employees, make certain they motivate, not intimidate.

Notes

Chapter Two

"What We've Got Here is a Failure to Communicate"

Paul Newman, Cool Hand Luke ~ 1967

It's no secret – or at least it shouldn't be – that communication is a key element in any relationship. It not only keeps us on the same page, but on the same planet. Small wonder then that problems arise quickly and grow out of proportion when communication is lacking or totally nonexistent--and even when it's staring them in the face, some people just don't get it.

> *"We know that communication is a problem,*
> *but the company is not going*
> *to discuss it with the employees."*
> ~ Fortune 500 Company Supervisor ~

Yes, even intelligent people really think that way. People really *say* those things. And people eventually feel like idiots when they realize how they have lapsed and could have benefited from a second look, a second thought—or a simple change of attitude. Words are powerful; and ironically enough, the shortest phrase can often have the strongest punch. For example:

I'm Sorry...

...probably the two most important words in resolving conflict—and the perfect armor for defusing a bad situation that could escalate to volatile. Enter stage left: the most irate customer you have ever seen. And he's headed your way. You've already made eye contact so there's no escaping the encounter—not that you'd run and hide, right? But at this point your only weapons are body language and communication. With the proper greeting, handshake, eye contact, serious listening, and (once he pauses to take a breath) the first words out of your mouth being "I'm sorry," you are on the right track. In all truth, no one really likes to apologize; and in this instance saying *I'm sorry* is not an admission of guilt. Ninety-nine percent of the time it most likely will not be your own personal problem, not a situation of your own creating. But you're representing your company, your management, your position, *and* yourself; and right now you are the only connection the customer has between his problem and what he hopes will be a solution. A sincere *I'm sorry* is empathy, pure and simple. Emphasis on sincere. It lets the customer know you understand his frustration, that you can put yourself in his place, you can see the issue from his perspective, and you'll do whatever can be done to remedy the situation. Small words, big impact.

An apology is the superglue of life.
It can repair just about anything.
~ Lynn Johnston ~

An apology is a good way to have the last word.
~ Anonymous ~

Two somewhat opposing takes on the apology issue—but regardless of which side of the *I'm-sorry* fence you're on, the words themselves build a winning resolution.

Are There Dumb Questions?

Well, no—there's no such thing as a dumb question. So often I've been approached by someone who says "I have a stupid question"—when I have always felt that the only stupid thing about questions is *not* asking them. Taking it a step further, there are definitely dumb ways to respond to questions. Examples:

➤ A person calls the library and says "do you have any books?" and the librarian replies, "nope, but if you call back tomorrow, we may get some in." Obviously, the person is really asking if they have a particular book...it just didn't come out quite right. Hopefully the response was an attempt at humor.

➤ A person arrives at a bowling alley and says, "Can I bowl?" and the service attendant says, "I don't know, can you?" What the person was really asking was when lanes would be available.

Help your staff anticipate the out-of-the-ordinary questions and rehearse the answers.

"Common sense is of paramount importance in business and customer service."
~ Anonymous ~

Listen, *Really* Listen

Listening is an art—a lost one at times, but nonetheless a remarkable skill. In relation to the examples cited above, at the most demanding moments it is required that you listen *beyond* the words in order to hear what is *not* being said. It is believed that people have two ears and one mouth for good reason. Have you ever had a conversation with someone and you knew darn well that they weren't listening? How often do *you* really listen? In the service industry, listening is the key; and interestingly enough, you can learn a lot by doing so. Don't worry; if you listen really well, you'll get your turn to talk later. And the benefits are significant. An improvement in listening skills creates better communication, which leads to better customer relationships, which allows you to better understand what the customer wants and needs. This puts you in the perfect position to better serve your customer, gaining their satisfaction, loyalty, and retention.

> *"Knowing your customers' need,*
> *will shape the vision to get there"*
> ~ Vinnie R. Panicker ~

The key to listening is being in the moment with your customers. Watching their body language. Looking them directly in the eye. *Really* hearing them. A great way to show a customer that you are focused and truly listening is to repeat a portion of what they have told you—echoing equals interest. "What I hear you saying is that ...." or "Just to confirm your expectations, they are ..."

Then there are those *wasted* questions, the answers to which are usually ignored—often empty rhetoric rather than actual interest or request. While a basic part of polite customer service "speech," some service providers seldom pay complete attention to the customer's response to:

- ➢ How are you today?
- ➢ Did you need something?
- ➢ How may I help you?

The number one rule for all of the above is if you're going to *ask*, then really *listen*.

Humor

During a lengthy hospitalization, my Dad was having a problem with persistently low blood pressure. For two nights, we had struggled for it to be over 75. One night the nurse came into his room and said "Mr. Johnson, I just don't know what I am going to do with you. You know, we really need to get this blood pressure up. If we can't, I'm going to have to do something drastic." Everyone in the room froze. She said "If we can't get it any higher, I'm just going to have to show you your hospital bill. I know that will definitely get it up!" We all laughed, even my Dad, and we felt the first sense of relief since he'd been admitted.

There is room for humor in almost every industry, in most situations. One local construction company gives a fortune cookie to each of their customers; but instead of the typical fortune or saying, inside the cookie is a joke. The company rep that I spoke with said that their own workers never hesitate to ask, "Aren't you going to give me *my* fortune cookie? I could use a good laugh too!"

What humor can you bring to your company?

Include Everyone in Your Conversation

Our cat Madison (all eighteen pounds of him) goes to the groomer about every six weeks. As soon as we arrive, they always say, "Well, hello Madison, we are so glad you are here today." Although Madison couldn't care less (and really doesn't want to be there), it is important to *me* that they remember us and have taken time enough to get to know us and call us by name.

While we go over how we would like Madison cut, the groomer will pet him and include him in the conversation. Perhaps you have to be an animal lover to understand that. Yes, he is a cat, but to us he is important. To them, he is important too. Remember, really, *Madison* is their customer.

At a local daycare, when children arrive for the day there is always someone at the door to greet them with a high five. Their next step is to welcome the parent. The children are pumped, the parents are confident to leave them in such great hands, and everyone—short or tall—is happy with the direction their day is heading.

Who do you need to include in your conversation? You know the obvious but think about those who are *not* so obvious...maybe someone on the sidelines who is just as much a part of the situation as your primary customer or contact.

Do Not Talk *Behind* our Back ~ OR ~ in *Front* of our Back

At the salon where I get my nails done, most of the employees speak English as a second language. But there is one difference between my current salon and those that I no longer patronize: they speak English 100% of the time. The staff there has said that they know it appears they may be speaking negatively of the customers when they converse in a language foreign to us. (Remember—the customer's perception.) And because of this, we were shocked one day as an employee approached another staff member and began talking to her in a foreign (to us) language. She had only gotten about ten words into her sentence when she immediately looked up at both of us and said "I am so sorry. I am so used to speaking in our language that sometimes it just comes out. I just didn't want you to think that we were talking about you."

"Information" OR "No Information" Desk

Arriving with a few minutes to spare for my scheduled presentation, I was relieved to see that friendly sign, "Information Desk." Traffic had been snarled, the directions I'd been given hadn't been the best, and I was unfamiliar with the building. Thank goodness there was a customer service saint waiting to save me. I approached the desk with a smile and asked for the room number where my seminar was being held. The saint peered at me over the magazine she was reading and said "I don't know anything about any rooms, don't know anything about a seminar" before her face disappeared behind the cover again. What? I felt my smile wilting. Aren't you an information desk? Not only did she not know anything, but she made no offer or attempt to get the information for me. Obviously, the saint of gossip magazines had more important things to do.

"Maybe 'Customer Service' should be more than one department."
~ SAP Ad ~

Exactly. And in my opinion, *any* desk or work area that you approach is an information desk, whether it bears that sign or not. If someone is sitting there who works for the company, they should be able to acquire any information that you need. If they don't know the answer, they're totally capable of finding someone who does. It is that simple.

Q. If you go to the staff at the resource desk of a library, what do you think their role is? **A.** To help you find resources.

To point to the resource material is not enough. The person should take you there, open the first book, show you the options, and let you know that their job is to assist you in any way you need. What is the resource person doing that is more important than helping the customer? If the resource person does not wish to help the patron, then maybe we do not need a resource person.

Let your staff know that they are all (figuratively) sitting at the company's information desk.

Body Language ~ The Eyes Have It

> *"Feelings are 55% body language,*
> *38% tone and 7% words."*
> ~ Grant M. Bright ~

The total impact of body language will be covered in more depth in a later section, but for now it's all in the eyes. During my father's hospital stay, his IV drip machine kept beeping; and when I say "kept beeping," I mean as soon as they would fix it, fifteen seconds later it would malfunction again and the incessant beeping would return. Each and every time the nurse would come into the room with a smile on her face, apologize, restart the medicine, watch it for a minute, then leave the room. After at least a dozen reruns of this identical routine, she decided that air bubbles were causing the trouble and she changed the medication bag to alleviate the problem. After that, the beeper never went off again.

We were surprised to see her just ten minutes later when she peeked into our room. She said "I was just checking to make sure the machine was working and—well frankly, I just missed seeing all of you." She consistently went beyond our expectations and made a tense situation bearable—handling it all with grace and compassion.

The next night we began experiencing the same problem, only with a different nurse on duty. Each time the nurse came to my father's room, she would roll her eyes, express her displeasure with being interrupted, and sigh... loudly. After beating on the machine, she sighed again (VERY loudly), grabbed the machine, and pulled it out of the room. About five minutes later she returned with the machine, plugged it in, and off she went.

Her body language and eye rolls set the mood for that entire evening. We felt uncomfortable and intimidated, that we were being inconsiderate and putting the nurse out when, in fact, the machine not working was not our fault at all. How could it be? Her poor attitude became even more obvious the next evening when our first nurse stopped by "just to see how things were." She wasn't even our duty nurse that evening but simply wanted to check on the family she had learned so much about the night before.

Have you ever asked your teenager to take out the trash and get the famous eye roll in reply? What you'd like to do to the teenager at that moment should not be written here. Have you ever been at a restaurant, returned your steak because it wasn't cooked properly, and gotten the same look from the waitress? Maybe *that* reaction shouldn't be put in words either. Sometimes people are simply not aware of what they are doing, and body language *can* be misinterpreted. But there is no room in the service industry for eye rollers, and if you're guilty of the habit it's one you should make an effort to lose. Acknowledging a customer immediately and consistently with correct and respectful eye contact is the answer.

A friend of mine told me the story of a *memorable* waitress they had while dining out one evening. She was nice enough while taking their order, writing down every detail— even the "can I get extra sour cream" and "can I get steak sauce." But when the time came for the actual dinner service, while she served all the correct food to each correct customer, she had forgotten the additional requests. When they asked again if they could please have those items, the waitress rolled her eyes and walked away. Rolled her eyes? Excuse me? I remember my niece getting *grounded* for rolling her eyes. Do customers ever deserve that type of behavior? Absolutely not. And any reputable company would consider it to be a totally inappropriate reaction...so unless you're fainting, no eye rolling allowed.

If you've lapsed in the past, rolled your eyes at a customer even one time, this can be your friendly reminder. In simplest definition it is an insult, a physical "oh brother." It is a reaction that turns body language into a game of charades, acting out negative emotions instead of a song, book or movie. But unfortunately the answer is so much easier to guess and it is just no fun at all. So think of it as another "do unto others" moment. You would not want to be on the receiving end of those ocular gymnastics, so please do not be the sender.

Taking a giant leap from overactive eyeballs to "where'd they go?"—have you ever walked by someone who was staring at the ground? Or sat across the desk from someone who seemed to be concentrating on the cosmic mystery of their shoelaces? Eye contact, done correctly, can say so much—and there are times when the lack of it can say even more. But it *is* a fine line. Correct eye contact involves looking directly at the other person's eyes, with smooth and appropriate glances away. It conveys a sense of interest in and connection to both the person and the subject being discussed. Excessive and incorrect eye contact results in staring, which can be creepy and intimidating—or connecting then looking away quickly (furtive and questionable)—or the complete inability to look someone in the eyes (frustrating). Practice your eye contact with someone. Try not to giggle. Get to the place where you feel comfortable and then be conscious of your eye contact.

Telephone Techniques

Before you apply for a driver's license, you study, you log driving hours, and you practice for months. If you're a high school-aged first-time driver, you also relent to the rigors of your Driver's Ed instructor as you learn rules of the road, state laws, and safe driving techniques before you are finally tested. So why shouldn't we ask those employees who answer the telephone to have some training too? Granted, not that many lives are endangered by poorly trained phone personnel, but still. How about when you call a vendor and they answer the telephone, "Yeah". (Believe me, it has happened.) Sometimes people don't understand that the simple act of answering the telephone is an extremely important one since it provides the first impression of the business. Here are some things to consider when answering the telephone:

➢ Develop a consistent tag line for your company. You may call a company five times in five days and have the telephone answered five different ways. Is this wrong? Well, mostly yes. When the telephone is answered, we should be fully aware of what company we are calling and who is answering the telephone. The greeting should be posted on each and every phone so that all staff members answer consistently.

➢ Enunciate all words. How many times have you called someone only to hear something along the lines of "XYZCompanycanwehelpyou"? What? E-nun-ci-ate. Make sure that your words are spoken in a way to be clearly heard and under-stood. I know, you have answered the telephone thousands of times but we still need to under-stand what you are saying.

➢ Decide what you want the first impression to be. A smiling, friendly voice is a great start. Many people believe that you can, to some extent, "hear" a smile in a person's voice. A friend of mine once worked with a woman who kept a small mirror on her desk by the phone; and every time she picked up the receiver, she smiled at herself in the mirror before she answered. It was a good-hearted source of humor to her co-workers, but she sure made a lot of those sales. So, answer the phone with a smile in your voice.

➢ Re-record your voicemail often. Make it fresh.

➢ Answer the phone within the first two rings (the first if you can).

➢ Always ask, "Is there anything else that I can assist you with today?"

➢ Change the telephone ring to accommodate the business. For example, if the person answering the phone is right there, a small ding might be more appropriate than a loud ring. At a casino, the phones all ring with the sound of slot machines. At a church, the phones ring with church bells. At a dog groomer, the phone barks. Be creative.

➢ Be sure to say everything clearly; even if you say the same thing over and over, you should always sound interested.

➢ Call in to your own company and see how the phone is being answered. You may be very surprised.

➢ The hold time should be productive for the caller. Hawaiian music doesn't do much of anything to improve business (unless you're a travel agent) but utilizing that time with a recorded promo-tion of your products is a great use of hold time and a positive marketing tool.

Use these tips to bring your telephone etiquette to the next level.

Appropriate Time for Employee Conversations

I do understand that there are times when two employees need to talk to each other. But when a customer approaches them the conversation needs to stop (even if they are in the middle of a sentence) and their focus should shift firmly to the customer. I hear it all – boyfriend problems, how much they hate their job, school homework—and as I stand waiting until they finish their conversation I begin to lose patience. It's not that I don't care—I do; but if a customer is waiting, work is the first priority.

While going through the checkout at my local super-market, it is interesting to hear the checker and the bagger having a conversation. Am I invisible? Do they not see me? I'm sure the same thing has happened to you. Here's an idea! What about having a conversation with *us*, the customers? I've never been a me-too-me-too kind of person, but I shouldn't have to be an uncomfortable and accidental audience when I'm really an intentional profit to their business.

There are also the inappropriate conversations. While I was waiting in the lobby of a law firm, I couldn't help but overhear the receptionist and a co-worker bad mouthing their employer. During their conversation, I heard one of them say "They expect me to answer all of these stupid telephone lines and wait on stupid people." Stupid people? Was she talking about me? If there were no people in their lobby, stupid or brilliant, would she still have a job?

While I was in line at a local fast food restaurant, the person in front of me presented a coupon after the clerk had completed ringing up the order. It was obvious that the clerk was upset and did everything in his power just to get the customer out of there. Once the customer finished the transaction and stepped away, lucky me, I was next. Instead of focusing on me, the employee turned to a co-worker and said "These people think we can read their minds. They should just give me the freaking coupon when they place their order." I continued to stand there. Then he said, "Yeah, can I take your order?"

One of the worst faux pas is for a manager to have a negative conversation with an employee, in front of not only fellow employees but customers as well, where everyone can hear. While in the waiting room at my doctor's office, I overheard the doctor telling the receptionist "I thought I told you that I didn't want to see any appointments after lunch. You are so stupid." You could just see the look of embarrassment on her face. I felt badly for both of them, the receptionist *and* the doctor—the receptionist because of her embarrassment, the doctor because apparently he had never taken a Management 101 class.

Please be cognizant of your private conversations by keeping them private.

Notes

Notes

Chapter Three

In a Manner of Speaking

Thank Your Customers

Is it really enough to say "thank you for coming in?" In some cases, absolutely. But when you want to be the best, you have to do it a little differently. Here are some ways to thank them:

> ➢ Handwritten "thank you" note ~ This would be appropriate when you have met with them personally. The note should include something specific about your meeting. For example: "It was a pleasure talking with you today about your need for additional insurance. Your son, Bob, is really growing up. I remember him when he was just a little boy..."

> ➢ Bounce back coupon ~ You can include this coupon as a way to thank them for coming and also to encourage them to return.

> ➢ Phone call ~ A friend of mine was looking for a dentist so I referred her to Dr. Davis. A few days after her visit I received a call from Dr. Davis (yes, Dr. Davis himself) thanking me for the referral and to see how I was doing.

> ➢ Speaking of referrals, be sure to thank those who make referrals to your company. I sent a bouquet of flowers to someone who referred a new client to me. She was overwhelmed with the flowers, calling me as soon as they had arrived. There is no way that I could have acquired a meeting with that client if it had not been for her. Guess how many additional clients she has sent my way? Over two dozen to date.

There are endless ways to say "thank you".

But I Don't *Want* to Smile

Someone once asked me "Can you teach someone to smile"? I think you can teach people anything they want to learn. If you are interviewing someone for a frontline position and throughout the entire interview they do not smile, that is a sign. Yes, they may be nervous, but your first impression of them could easily be the same one they pass along to the customers.

So—what if you have already *hired* the person and it's only now that you realize they seldom smile? I would first begin by addressing the smiling (or lack thereof). Sometimes people are not even aware that they are not smiling. During a training session, someone once told me "I am too busy to smile". If you are truly that busy, you *should* be smiling. That means business is good. Think about what makes you smile. For me:

- ➤ A picture of my niece Bailey
- ➤ A picture of Barry Manilow
- ➤ Thinking of one of my dad's bad jokes
- ➤ A Toby Keith song

The list is endless. So, when I am having a bad moment (or day), I pull one of those from the emergency kit and remind my face what a smile feels like.

Make a list of what makes *you* smile. Stick that list by your telephone—or in your wallet—or anywhere that you can easily access. Use the list when you need to smile. It's likely that you are not smiling 24/7, but if you are in the service industry (and if you really think about it, we all are) then you need to be smiling. Smile lines are better badges of valor than frown lines.

Whose Hand Do You Want Me to Shake?

You find yourself in a situation where you want to make an impression that will knock the person's socks off. My recommendation for the very best beginning is a nice, solid handshake. The perfect handshake does and says so much, communicating character and personality in only a few seconds' time. And you want to be certain that yours explains exactly who and what you are. The ideal handshake:

- ➤ Thumb facing the sky
- ➤ Four fingers straight ahead, forming a 90 degree angle from the thumb to the index finger
- ➤ Firm grip (but not *too* firm)
- ➤ Make direct eye contact

- ➢ Smile
- ➢ Greet the person

What can go wrong with a handshake?
- ➢ Too firm of a handshake (cuts the blood flow from the other person's hand or crushes their knuckles)
- ➢ Too wimpy of a handshake (says you are not confident)
- ➢ Dirty hands (says you don't take care of yourself) – If you are in a profession for which your hands are always dirty, have some moist towelettes handy and apologize when you shake hands. If I were dealing with a mechanic who started out by shaking my hand, looking me in the eye and greeting me, they would have made a great first impression.
- ➢ Great handshake, but with no eye contact or greeting (try it, it just doesn't work)

There are several other options for handshakes. I have heard from many seniors that instead of a handshake they would prefer that the person take their hand and simply touch or grasp it for a moment. In other instances, some people are just not hand shakers at all. Some feel it is unsanitary, some feel it is not always appropriate; but in most situations, the handshake *is* appropriate and makes you stand out. Think about it. If you went to the library and as soon as you arrived, the desk clerk stood up, shook your hand and said (quietly) "Hi, my name is Sue, welcome to our library. If I can assist in any way, please let me know." First of all, you would probably be flabbergasted. But, would this library stand out? Would you think they had excellent customer service? You bet.

Do you want to see this in action? Stop by Sue's Corner in Granite City, Illinois. My mom and sister own this bar, and they introduce themselves to every new person who comes in the door. They take the time to walk over, shake the patron's hand, and present themselves. They explain that the bar is family owned and welcome them to the establishment. And when the customer leaves, they always thank him or her for coming in. When is the last time you went to a bar and the owner came over to extend a personal introduction? Next time you're in the neighborhood, stop by and tell them Dawn sent you.

How do I know this works? Whenever I am training in the Granite City area, I always include a few customer service examples from the bar. On many occasions people have told me "I've been in that bar and they really *do* that." Point made. The handshake is memorable, and it can make not only a good *first* impression but a lasting one as well.

How is your handshake? Don't be so quick to think that you can't shake hands at your place of business. If it's not a standard part of the service *now*, there's no better time to start.

Perception

Wow! Perception is reality. You don't believe me? Consider this. You are giving a speech for a women's group. Two women in the front row cross their arms at the beginning of your speech, make no eye contact with you whatsoever, and actually start and continue a conversation between themselves during your talk. What is your perception? Are they bored? Inconsiderate? Do they have an attitude? Did it change the way you spoke to them? Were you angry? Maybe, but reality is that both were freezing and were simply discussing whom they might contact about turning off the vent that was blowing cold air right on top of them.

I actually had this happen to me and I later used it in a role play example. Someone raised their hand and said, "But they were cold." I said, "Then they needed to get a jacket, (or raise their hand and call attention to the problem so they could not only comfortably enjoy the seminar, but not be a distraction to it). Perception was reality, and her perceived attitude made the rest of the group uncomfortable."

An example: One of my best students was going back to school to become a paralegal having already received her nursing degree. The opportunities for her future were endless. A paralegal who has medical knowledge? She potentially could make six figures.

She was in her last semester and ready to graduate so she decided to put together her resume, cover letter, references, and portfolio. I assisted her with all of that information; and the end result was one of the best portfolios I had ever seen. We reviewed potential interview questions, discussed interview dress, and I figured she could call her own job.

After several interviews she noticed that she had not been called back. I couldn't figure it out. So, prior to her next interview she stopped by to see me to show me some changes she had made on her resume. She came in looking absolutely dazzling—perfect business suit, manicured hands, polished shoes, and...well...an earring in her nose.

I asked, "When did you get the nose ring?"

"Oh, I just don't wear it to school but I wear it everywhere else," she said.

"Well," I said, "I think I just discovered the reason you are not getting your jobs. Most attorney offices are conservative and they need people who can interact well with their conservative clients. I doubt they find your nose ring conservative. Did they ever ask you about it?"

She was quiet for a minute then said. "Yes. And I told all of them that I would not remove the ring for anyone."

Okay...well...after *much* discussion she finally said, "I do not want to work for a company that will not let me wear a nose ring." Despite my arguments and explanations to the contrary, that's where we left it. I am not kidding when I tell you that two (yes, two) years later she was still looking for a job. When she called me, I explained to her that she was in a conservative arena and needed to either open her own law firm or get rid of the nose ring. She decided to finally ditch the nose ring, went on an interview and they hired her immediately.

I do understand the need to be yourself, to express your unique personality, but unless it can be done in a quiet and understated way, do it on your own time. When you're on the company's clock you need to represent *them* according to their policies, image, and expectations. Also, on the employer's side of the situation, you need to be up front about things like that. Today, in addition to piercings, many people have tattoos. If your policy is that tattoos cannot be visible, then you need to be straightforward about it, because I can guarantee that the issue will not go away. Explain it during the interview if possible. Don't wait to tell them until their first day. It could most likely be their last.

Body Language – The Sequel

So much is said without even speaking. Have you ever walked into a business and, simply by looking at the first employee you see, you know that you are regarded as more of an imposition than a customer? And yet they haven't said a word.

One of my biggest turn offs is crossed arms. To me, crossed arms illustrate "defensive." Some people disagree with me—they say they are just cold. In that case, I say get a sweater. I heard a phrase years ago that has stayed in my memory: "The message sent is the message heard." Logically translating, what that means is that if I perceive crossed arms to show defensiveness, then when someone assumes that stance they are defensive. So basically, perception is reality. The person crossing his arms needs to understand how he is perceived and make a change to correct the mixed signals. You may be calmly saying *one* thing while your body language is shouting another.

Where do we stand on posture? No pun intended. At a training session, I asked each participant to describe themselves using only one adjective. As I went around the room I heard things like *positive, relaxed,* and *dynamic.* When I reached the next participant I was sure that her adjective would be *negative.* You see, she had sat through the training for two hours with her arms crossed, no smile, and staring off into space. But her self-descriptive word choice was *happy.* Happy, I thought? So at the break I took a moment to talk with her. And guess what? She really *was* happy. So I asked her to trade places with me. I sat down in her chair and mimicked her exact appearance as I had seen it from my vantage point at the podium. You could tell that she was completely shocked.

So, we discussed posture, eye contact and facial expressions. Three days after the training I received a call from this person. She said "You have completely changed my life." As we began to talk, she said "People look at me completely differently now. They say that I look like a new woman." But her makeover had nothing to do with haircut or color, makeup or wardrobe—all we had changed was her body language. In her case, her self esteem had also been greatly enhanced, and makeovers don't come much better than that.

⚜

One day I entered a card shop where the owner was sitting behind the counter with her elbow on the table and her chin cupped in the palm of her hand. She did indeed make eye contact with me but did nothing else to change her position or demeanor. When I made my selections and walked to the counter, she was still in the same position. She waited for me to set my purchases on the counter before she slowly drug herself out of the chair and let out a yawn. Without *saying* a word, she clearly told me that she didn't care. Remember, she didn't have to *say* a word—body language said it for her.

Along those same lines, another strong example comes from the time I was asked to substitute at a local college. The class was very participative and I really enjoyed the evening. After the class, the teacher called me to see how it went. I told her how much I had enjoyed how actively the class had participated in what we had covered that day and she said, "I sure don't know what you did to get them to talk. I ask them and ask them, and no one wants to participate." After that class, she asked if I would come back to class to give her some feedback.

The next week I stopped by her class and observed her, and the most telling characteristic was that during the entire class she stood with her arms folded. After class she said, "See what I mean? No one said a word". I asked her about the folded arms and she said, "That classroom is always cold." So, the next class I asked her to be conscious of her arms, leaving them at her side (and to put on a sweater). She was amazed. Almost from the beginning she was getting class participation. See, her body language was saying "closed" and "not listening". She had built a body language wall between herself and her students and she had absolutely no idea.

Are you aware of your body language? I had a training participant say to me "I fold my arms – that's just the way it is!" That's fine, but perception is reality. If people perceive you as being closed off, then reality is (perception is) that you are closed off. Remember, you can only change yourself. Why not take an inventory of your body language by asking others how they perceive it.

What does your body language say?

Be "In the Moment"

Of all the "in the moment" examples that I have, this may by far be the best. I was checking out at a local grocery store, piling my groceries onto the conveyer belt. All fifty-four items (totaling $81.15) were scanned and then bagged by the checker. I processed my debit card and then realized that, up until this moment, the checker had made zero conversation with me. There was no "hello," no "how are you," no "these brownies look good." Nothing. In fact, no one in the store had acknowledged me at all. I had encountered several store employees without any notice whatsoever.

After I processed my debit card I turned to the checker and said, "Aren't you even going to say 'thank you'?" He tore off the receipt, handed it to me, and said "It's on the bottom of your receipt." Oh my goodness! I had to take a moment to catch my breath. I really thought I was on Candid Camera.

So, I decided to write to the president of the company, explaining my experience. I sent the letter, waited two weeks, but there was no reply. So, I sent letter two (with letter one attached), describing the incident once again. Still no reply. So, I typed up letter three (with letters one and two attached) and noted "I now understand that the nut doesn't fall far from the tree. The words 'customer service' are non-existent in your and your staff's vocabulary. Poor service begins right at the top, and I will never again shop at any of your stores."

I have told that story to thousands and thousands of people. The story itself is almost unbelievable. Everyone says, "The least he could have said is 'hello.'" Yes, that is the least, but why are we thinking about the least? I don't know of too many people who strive to be the *least* in their profession. Let's create another version--what I think *should* have happened.

As soon as the previous customer was taken care of, the checker should have made eye contact with me, smiled and said, "I'm sorry about your wait" (no matter how long the wait). As I began placing my items on the conveyer belt, he could have started with "Did you find everything you needed?" (If I indicated that I did not, he should find someone who could assist me and acquire the item I was unable to find. The reason that question often goes unasked is that they do not want to hear, "No, I didn't find everything." That only complicates their job by creating more work.) He should also take a look at my cart to see if there are things that I might be able to leave in the cart that he could simply scan.

Then he could continue to scan my items and make small talk by being observational. Maybe make a general observation. "So, are you a big St. Louis Cardinals fan?" Maybe I have a child with me. The checker could address the child and say, "Hi, how are you today?" What if it is obvious that I could use assistance to my vehicle? Instead of asking, an offer of assistance from the bagger would be the perfect gesture.

The checker should continue to be in the moment. Does the customer need a pen? Do they need you to hold the receipt while they sign it? Does the person need assistance placing the bags into the cart? If no bagger is available, the checker should assist putting the groceries in the cart. (I know it is easier to stand behind the counter, but remember, we want to be great.) As I begin to leave, thank me for visiting your store and let me know that you will look forward to my next visit.

Another checkout story...as I finalized a purchase at a local department store, I explained to the checker that I had two transactions, one as a personal purchase and one for my company. So, he rang up the first order and I used my credit card. Once I swiped my credit card, the checker asked to see my driver's license. So, I showed it to him; and he rang up the second transaction. I then used my *company* credit card. After swiping it, he surprised me by asking to see my driver's license AGAIN. I said, "I haven't changed; I have been standing right here." He said, "It's store policy. I need to see it." To this day, I believe that checker had no idea I was the same person. He was totally detached, *out* of the moment, and just going through the motions like a robot.

Watching news interviewers on TV, you can easily tell when they are not in the moment. If you watch them, you can identify when they are thinking about the next question, and when they are actually listening to the answer. You probably know exactly who I am talking about.

✤

I knew a gentleman who worked at a place where they sang "Happy Birthday" to all customers who were celebrating, or trying to ignore, their special day. People came from miles—just so they could embarrass their friends with the public serenade. When all eight employees were singing "Happy Birthday," I couldn't help but notice one employee who performed with a huge smile on his face. The employee actively involved the birthday person by looking him in the eye, shaking his hand, and congratulating him. After the event was over, I stopped the employee to ask what kept him so happy. He said, "The person having the birthday is what is important. I try to keep myself in the moment at all times. If you don't stay in the moment, you miss so much."

✤

My niece has always enjoyed coming to Aunt Dawn and Uncle Ted's house. Every time she visits, we plan a fun and usually exhausting array of events from cooking and playing games to fishing, shopping, and so much more. Each and every time she visits, we bake something. When she was two, she could use the wooden spoon to stir. When she was four, she could begin pouring in the ingredients. When she was six, she measured things. When she was eight, we decided she could use the mixer. What a big day for an eight-year old.

To give you a little background, we do not just bake. We BAKE. Two weeks before she arrives, I head to the grocery store and start scouting for supplies. I buy all of the ingredients as well as sprinkles, cookie cutters, toppings, decorations, etc. It is a big day...and I look forward to her visit as much, if not more so, than she does. So, when the big day arrived, she was so excited because she knew she was finally going to graduate to using the mixer. We talked about safety issues and the best way to keep her fingers out of the mixer. We are all pumped up, and she is ready to start.

I am putting away the dishes, washing the floor, and cleaning out the microwave. In the meantime, Bailey is mixing away, talking about something (I couldn't tell you what it was). As I reach down into the dishwasher, something hits me on the head. I reach up and discover that it's batter. I look over at Bailey, who has been talking while mixing. As she was talking, she was raising the mixer out of the bowl and batter was flying all over the kitchen. And all over me. "Bailey!" I yelled, and nearly scared her to death. She dropped the mixer, but the batter kept flying. I finally just unplugged the mixer and everything stopped. Everything. Dead silence. Until I began laughing. I realized that I had looked forward to this moment for two weeks and yet couldn't tell you a thing that happened. Guilty as charged...I wasn't in the moment. I missed her conversation. I missed her mixing "skills." I missed everything about that moment... except the batter in my hair.

What does this have to do with customer service? Everything. You should be in the moment with your customer. You should be in the moment with everyone in your life. The time is now. You've heard it before but it bears repeating: this is not a dress rehearsal for life, this is the real thing.

Another "in the moment" story? Okay. My husband, my sister, her boyfriend, and I fly to Las Vegas. We are out there for one fabulous week so that I can secret shop for a casino. On our last night there, Barry Manilow is at the Hilton. You know I have never missed a Barry concert so I sure wasn't going to miss this one. I couldn't talk anyone into going with me (imagine that), so I went online to buy the best ticket available. It didn't matter how much I paid (and I paid dearly). I arrived at the Hilton alone and walked into the concert hall. When I presented my ticket to the usher she said, "Oh, you are on stage." I said, "No, I purchased this ticket online and wanted to be right in the front row." So, up the stairs we go, to THE STAGE. Oh my goodness. I am on stage—with Barry—just five feet from his piano. I couldn't believe it.

As I sat there in disbelief, I called my mom. I told her where I was and that I was right next to his piano. She said, "Dawn, just don't hurt him." After I got off the phone with mom, I said, "I want to enjoy this moment, right here, right now." I began to smell the air, take in the stage decorations, and watch the people; absorbing every fraction of my surroundings. To this day, I remember how that concert *smelled*. I remember the passion that he put into his songs. I remember leaving the hall that evening with a filled-to-the-brim sense of satisfaction.

Each day I realize how important it is to live in the moment. You can live in the moment with your customers by really listening to what they have to say and paying attention. Trust me on this – you will not regret it. Figure out what it is going to take to be in the moment with each and every customer you encounter.

Manners – Are They Teachable?

"The greatest teacher teaches only once—to a
child, or to a grownup past hope."
~ Anonymous ~

One of my client companies has been recognized and honored, at both the company and staff levels, by receiving some of the highest customer service awards in the industry. His company accepts complaint calls 24 hours/7 days per week; and in addition to his outstanding customer service policies, he always seems to hire the right people. How is that possible? I sat down with him one day to discuss how he consistently manages to select and hire the right people. He was kind enough to share the details of his interview process.

Two Tuesdays a month their company interviews eight people. The candidates are asked to arrive at the company by 9:45 a.m. for a 10:00 a.m. interview. They are to park on the parking lot where they are greeted by an attendant. When the interviewees arrive, the attendant documents the details of attitude, behavior, and their general treatment by the candidates. Do the interviewees talk down to the parking attendant? Do they say "thank you"? Were they on time? When the interviewees enter the building they are greeted by the receptionist, who rates them as well.

At 10:00 a.m., the receptionist asks the interviewees to all take the elevator to the 14th floor. A casually dressed gentleman also gets on the elevator. When the elevator reaches the 4th floor, the gentleman sneezes. What is he waiting for? For someone to say "God bless you." You guessed it— he is the company CEO; and between the parking lot attendant and the receptionist, they have—and *he* has—just conducted 50% of the interview process. His theory behind the exercise is that a person's manners in a casual encounter will also be an automatic extension in a professional situation. So when an employee is dealing with a complaint call at 2:00 A.M. and the complainant sneezes, he is assured that the customer will receive the additional courtesy of a "bless you." By the time the interviewees get off the elevator, they have little idea that their interview is half over, and that they've already received a pass or fail on that part of it. It's an amazing concept.

None of us can count the "aggravating" parental nudges we received as children: *mind your manners*. But if we're lucky, some of them stuck—and carried over into our adult worlds. It's such a simple thing and the opportunities are endless: *thank you, have a nice day, enjoy the beautiful weather...* Perhaps your company has a consistent greeting (when the customer arrives and when the customer leaves). If not, pump up the customer service and create your own.

❦

Our Chamber of Commerce office is located in what was originally a residence. Everyone who walks into our "home" is greeted as the door is opened for them, one of us shakes their hand and offers them something to drink. Why do we do this? First of all, we want people to feel welcome. Whatever reason has brought them to our office, we want them to feel like the Chamber is a great place to visit. Also, our goal is to be "the best," not the *least*, and this is just one step in the process.

So back to the original question, are manners teachable? Well, yes, I believe they are. It seems much easier to teach a child than an adult, but it can be done.

Let's start with "Thank you" or "Thank you and have a great day." If your expectation for your staff is to say one of these phrases, then practice with them on appropriate timing, actual tone, speed of phrase, etc. It is not fair to simply tell your staff "I expect you to say this every time." Work with them on how you envision it. Then, the first time they do it, tell them "great job." Help them feel comfortable with the phrase and before long it will come naturally. Let's say that you have an employee who refuses to do this. Well, that is why you include "proper manners" in your expectations. It becomes easier for you as a manager to hold people accountable.

How about opening the door for people? Yes, I know what you are saying, "but it should come naturally." Yes, I completely agree that it should; but believe me, I have seen many people who could use a crash course in manners. Make certain your staff is aware of your expectations on opening doors. But your staff doesn't have *time* to open the front door like we do? In some cases, I absolutely understand. But there are companies that could easily put this action in place today. Think about it. If you were walking up to a company, and as you approached the door an employee opened it for you, wouldn't you be impressed? Why not put your customers in awe? Do something that sets you apart. It's all about the WOW.

The list is endless. Holding the elevator open. Opening the car door. Holding an umbrella. Saying "God bless you." Offering to assist someone with a wheelchair (but be sure to ask if they would like assistance). Saying "thank you for the opportunity to serve you today." Hanging up their coat. Saying "have a nice day." Some of the best salespeople I know have gained that level simply by having the best manners. Who wouldn't want to do business with someone who takes the time to pay personal attention to the details?

Storytime... We were at a networking event, where the simple common denominator in the purpose of attendance was to meet people. Out of 120 people present, four had earpieces on the entire time. So many people later told me that it made them uncomfortable to talk with those individuals. It was their perception that the person was more important than them. Also, was the person really sure if they were talking with them or someone on the other end? I understand how much time the earpieces save and their safety when driving, but people need to realize how this makes them appear to others. Basically, when people wear the earpieces, they are sending the message that "when this earpiece goes off, I will direct my conversation and attention to whomever is calling...not you." If that is *not* what they are saying, then they should consider removing their earpiece.

When you begin to train your staff and set the expectations for manners, remember, it is all in how you approach people, whether they will want to do as asked or not. Role play is a huge advantage, showing the staff firsthand how you expect them to show their manners. Also, you constantly serve as a role model whether you intend it or not, so be sure to check your own manners as well.

What other manners and protocol can you come up with that would be appropriate in your field? Are you setting a good example for your employees?

Networking

This is an art. But what does it have to do with customer service? Everything. My favorite networking example is this:

One of my favorite pizza parlors is Alfonzo's Pizzeria in Maryville, Illinois. The owner, Mike, could teach a class on networking with the customer. Mike visits every table, asking how things are, if they need anything, if it's their first visit to the restaurant, and he truly listens to what his customers have to say. What makes it so amazing is that he is not just blowing smoke—he is sincerely interested, he remembers things, and is continuously building relationships. And his memory is a long one, going back at least more than twenty years ago. I can only judge by a firsthand example:

In 2000, my sister and her friend went to Alfonzo's Pizzeria. As they were eating their dinner, Mike came over to ask how everything was. They said it was great. He then looked at my sister and said, "You and your parents and your older sister used to come here when you were younger, didn't you"? They both looked at each other and said "How do you remember that?" He said, "I remember your parents used to bring you here when you were a kid." Then he looked at my sister and said, "You used to love when I gave you those plastic rings." My sister said, "Yes, I used to think they were real diamonds!" Did I mention that my sister is now thirty? That was over twenty years ago...but he was paying attention. I'm certain he still is.

How can you get started with networking? Introduce yourself to everyone who walks in. Shake hands. Ask if they have been there before. Welcome them. Is your competitor doing that? If you want to be the best, you have to be better than your strongest competitor.

❦

When I was a kid growing up, we used to go to a local drive-up convenience store. The simple process was that you placed your order with someone, they went inside and got your order, then returned with your items. Once the transaction was made, they always followed up with a small piece of candy for the children in the car. Each time my parents needed to pick up something in town I would say, "Let's go to the place where they give candy." Many banks today give stickers and lollipops to kids or biscuit treats to dogs. Small gestures, but those banks and that convenience store often earn our business because of it.

A favorite butcher shop of mine gives away Little Smokies to each child who comes into their shop. The Smokies serve many purposes, one being the obvious—to give them a little something extra. It also helps them be patient during the wait while the order is filled. But the one relating to customer service actually targets customer retention, and helps the child remember to remind mom and dad which butcher shop is the best. Clever!

My Rolodex would knock your socks off. My cards actually fill two Rolodex holders, and I have a card on everyone I know. I make copious notes such as names of children, names of pets, and special interest items about the person on the back of the individual cards. Prior to calling them, I can refresh myself on their individual information. They are usually wowed, and I am *happy* they are wowed. It sure helps the networking thing, and everyone thinks I have a great memory. I just have a great Rolodex.

An example might be as follows: Bob and Sally Smith, address, phone, Bobby (12), likes baseball and soccer; Teri (5), likes dolls and her dog Max; both like yellow suckers.

Strive to be the best networker that you can be!

Notes

Notes

Chapter Four

"I Got a New Attitude"

Patti LaBelle, song lyrics ~ Circa 1984

No Whining

As the song goes, "The employees on the bus go whah whah whah." And they whine and whine and whine. It is amazing to me how many people spend their entire life whining. Poor me. Poor me. Instead of whining, why not invest the same effort into determining how you can get what you want.

I remember a friend of mine many years ago, constantly whining about not being able to find a good paying job. I suggested that she return to school, and she shot down that idea. I suggested that she find a trade, and she shot down that idea too. My friend eventually ended up working at a gas station, making minimum wage and whining her way through each and every day. "I don't get paid enough money" or "this is a thankless job." Some jobs *are*. But in a larger sense, the job is what you make it. If you want to do better, then you have to *be* better. In most instances, people get where they are because of hard work; and attitude is a huge part of it.

Ironically though, *being* better and *doing* better can bring opposing reactions. I have seen this happen countless times. A certain employee succeeds, and the others choose not to step up. What do you do? On the managerial level it is always important to recognize outstanding employees for their work. If all they see is the manager working with those who *aren't* getting it, and not acknowledging those who *do*, then the ones who are excelling really have nothing to work toward—and seemingly little incentive, other than self-accomplishment, to continue the superior work they're doing.

An additional downside is the predictability that the employee who gets it is most likely taking grief from those who are not trying. (Remember high school?) So, if you are the manager and you witness something of this nature, it needs to be addressed. There is absolutely no reason that the employee who is working so hard should be badgered and hassled by other employees who are just going through the motions with very little effort. Additionally, you should make sure that you, as a manager, are not contributing to the jealousy by repeated public acknowledgement of the outstanding employee. Public recognition is deserved, and credit should be given when justified—just do not do it constantly.

Gift Cards – Are They Really That Much Trouble?

We often use gift cards at the local discount store. There's one particular checker who apparently has a serious aversion to the whole process, and the minute he zeroes in on the gift card he begins the conversation with "Oh, not a gift card. I *hate* those things." You what? You hate us using a gift card that we have already purchased from your company? Are you crazy? All things considered, it appears that the employee has never been properly trained on redeeming the gift card, so each time he has to run it through the register, it's very trial and error. More training, less complaining.

"Work is either fun or drudgery.
It depends on your attitude. I like fun."
~ Colleen Barrett ~

Approach is Everything

"The obstacles you face are...mental barriers
which can be broken by adopting
a more positive approach."
~ Clarence Blasier ~

You have heard the saying "it is all in the approach." Well, no more needs to be said. The way you approach people has a great deal to do with the ultimate outcome of any given situation. How you approach someone has everything to do with how the rest of the conversation goes. For those untrained or unaccustomed to dealing with rude customers, the normal reflex is to be rude in return. Unfortunately, defense mechanism kicks in before sensibility.

I had a co-worker who constantly complained about the service at a small gas station. She was always telling me, "You need to get them as a client and train them on giving good service." But every time I frequented their business I received excellent service. One morning she called and said "Let's ride together so you can see what I mean." So off we went...with her feeling somewhat gratified that I would finally witness customer service at its poorest, and me just being curious.

We went into the gas station which was fairly busy with an early morning crowd. We both filled up our drinks and stepped to the checkout. She was ahead of me. In a snippy tone of voice she told the clerk, "Give me a pack of Marlboro cigarettes and two lottery tickets." The clerk set the cigarettes on the counter, printed out her lottery tickets and set them on the counter, rang her up, and gave her the change. No other conversation transpired. I approached the counter and the clerk said "Good morning." I said, "Good morning. Could I please have two tickets for tonight's lottery?" The clerk smiled and said, "How about if I print you out the two winning tickets and you can split the prize with yourself?" We both laughed. The clerk finished my transaction and said "Have a beautiful day out there and enjoy this weather." I said, "You too."

When we got into my car my friend said, "See what I mean? Did you see how the clerk treated me?" Needless to say, our conversation that followed was a long one. Proper approach needs to come from both directions. Try to imagine it as a *friendly* tennis match. A gentle serve may likely warrant a gentle return. But the volleys can come fast and furious. Evaluate your approach. If you consistently receive poor service, what or who is the common denominator?

Are You Happy That I am Here or Not?

"You are serving a customer, not a life sentence. Learn how to enjoy your work."
~ Laurie McIntosh ~

My husband and I had the opportunity to go away for a long-awaited weekend. We chose to travel in the off season, taking advantage of the lower prices and the beautiful

Christmas lights. Our trip coincided with the last weekend that the city was open prior to their closing for the winter.

We decided to take in a local comic show and called the club to see if we would need reservations. The person on the other end of the phone laughed and said "No, not this time of year." So we ventured off, looking forward to a great evening and a lot of laughs. When we arrived, we noticed that we were able to take any seat we wanted. In fact, in a place that usually holds over 1,000 people there were less than a hundred in the first few rows. We settled in our seat and got ready for the fun, thinking we'd enjoy it even more minus the crowd.

The comic came out and started with "Well hello, where is everybody?" Where is everybody? We are right here. He went on to say how much better his shows were when the club was full and that we shouldn't expect a lot—that he'd been doing this show all season and this was his last weekend. A joke or two later he told us that he was tired and really just didn't think he had it in him. Well, that certainly set the scene. All night we heard his litany of how the club was usually full and this was his off season. He even commented that some of his staff were not in the show so we were really not seeing the entire production. My husband and I were lucky enough to have a coupon for a slightly discounted ticket, but I wonder how that made the full price customers feel?

The point in telling this story is that no matter how tired he was or how many times he performed this show, we were there to see it. For us it was the first time—and we deserved to see the same show that the early-season guests had enjoyed. Why should ours be of lesser quality?

The show was mediocre at best, and we would never consider going back—not even during the peak season. We will also not recommend anyone seeing this comic again. We should have been the most important audience in his life *at that moment*. It was such a disappointment in an otherwise great weekend. But, we were left with a bad taste in our mouth, and it would take a lot to get it out of there.

Negativity – No Room in the Workplace

Negative people. They are everywhere. Do you realize that statistics cite that 20% of the people in the world are negative? That is one in five. In addition to those odds, I have found that negative people breed negative people. Are you with me on this?

Why do we hire negative people? Because they are taught to hide their negativism in the interview. Well, those days can end *now*. If you are an interviewer, change up the questions. Use emotion when describing and directing the questions and ask them in a way that elicits emotion from the interviewee. Be alert for negative body language, forced smiles, raised tone of voice. I once asked, in a very forceful tone, "What happened the last time your boss told you to do something you didn't want to do?" The interviewee said, "I told her she could do it herself!" The force of my voice and the change of the question caught her off guard and pushed her to respond with the real answer before she could think of an acceptable one that she had rehearsed. Clearly she was not a chosen candidate for our position.

So, what do you do about negative people? Well, frankly, I try my best not to spend a lot of time with them. It's a given that if you surround yourself with positive people, they will help you stay positive. If you surround yourself with negative people—well, you get the idea.

What if the majority of your co-workers are negative people? It's important to remember that no matter what, you are probably not going to change them...at least not without drastic measures. If it bothers you that much, you may want to consider finding another job. Also, the service that the group is providing (no matter *how* great and positive *your* service is) will be recognized as negative by many people. And you will be judged by those around you.

Identifying signs of a negative person:
➤ Whining
➤ Talking bad about customers (and they do not care who they tell)
➤ Talking bad about other employees
➤ Gossiping
➤ Negative body language
➤ Lack of initiative
➤ Refusal to listen to new and positive ideas
➤ Overly critical

Do any of those describe you? Based on statistics alone, I figure that one in every five who read this book has a symptom listed above. If you honestly want to know if any of those characteristics fit you, be brave enough to ask a co-worker who would tell you the truth. You can tell them you've come across an employee betterment quiz and would like to know if they've noticed you exhibiting any traits similar to those listed. When they say "yes" to any or all of them, your first reaction will probably be to knock them out. But step back. Take this constructive feedback and use it to your advantage. Take stock of what you can change.

"Treat everyone with respect and kindness.
Period. No exceptions."
~ Kiana Tom ~

One of the things that I have learned is that often what drives us crazy about others is what we do poorly ourselves. For example, my niece is ten and she is driven by a calendar. She needs to know *where* we are going, *when* we are going, and plans for the next two weeks. I said to both my sister and my Mom "It's crazy that she needs to know things in advance—she's ten!" They both went completely silent and looked at each other in disbelief. Finally my mom said, "Dawn, that is *you*. Bailey is you." Oh my goodness. She *is* me. "I must have driven people crazy all of my life," I said. They both shook their head. Hmmm.

❦

What negative effects occur when one customer hears you talking negatively of another customer? A friend and I were second in line at a fast food restaurant. The person ahead of us was ordering when another customer came up and said "Excuse me, but you didn't get my order right. I had onion rings instead of fries and diet soda, not regular." The clerk took the tray and didn't say a word, simply set it on the counter while he finished the order of the person he'd been waiting on. When he'd replaced the incorrect items and returned the tray to the customer, there we were...next in line, while the two clerks bounced verbal barbs back and forth. "Who does she think she is? We aren't here to be at her beck and call. She gets what she gets. Next?" I think both of us would have much preferred to leave, but aside from causing even more attention to the situation it would have been a crush to reverse the flow of the lunch crowd. So we reluctantly placed our order, trying to erase "she gets what she gets" from our memory cells and hoping that no *special sauce* was included on our burger.

There's at least one in every place of business, that person who always has something negative to say. Whether it's about the company, the boss or another employee, the words and attitude seem endless; and if left unchecked, they can breed and multiply. Again, negativity breeds negativity. But where does it come from and how do you deal with it? The source or cause can be as varied as the way it manifests itself. I'm certain you've had the occasion to hear (or *over*hear) one employee trash-talking another. One day while I was in line at a grocery store, I became an accidental audience to a conversation between the bagger and the checker. (Nope, I wasn't involved.) The checker said "See Bob over there. He is such a jerk to work with. He just stands around talking about everyone and doesn't do his work. It's so rude when he does that." I wanted to hand the guy a mirror, but I just thought "there's another one for my book."

I'm not a shrink, but we all know that people often speak badly of others to make themselves appear bigger and better. Low self esteem? Envy? Both? Regardless, the end result is the same. Or sometimes it's simply a matter of the person being bitter, soured on life and not finding much good in anything.

Many years ago I worked with Sally. Every day at 10:15 a.m. she would take a cigarette break, and even though I am a non-smoker I always went with her for my break as well. She would spend the entire ten minutes complaining about her boss, her kids, her husband, her workload, her co-workers, the weather, etc. And when the break was over, I felt nearly battered, thinking more negative thoughts than I could ever have managed on my own. Imagining problems where there weren't any. Then Sally went on vacation for a week—and during those breaks I sat with Kelly, who talked about how great things were, how lucky she was just to be alive, have a great job, have a great family, etc. I felt fantastic when I went back to work.

On Monday, Sally returned...but I never went on break with Sally again. I realized that she was pulling me in and wanted me to have a negative attitude like her—and I had let her pull me in for a long time. No more. My entire outlook on the job changed. Surround yourself with positive people and you will be positive. Surround yourself with negative people and you will be negative.

You have to be careful though. Sometimes a negative person will try to camouflage what is simply his own bad attitude and lure you into believing that it's his intellect and critical thinking that enables him to dissect and analyze the situation—thus becoming the *only* one who could possibly have the right answer. Too many good ideas are lost this way, shot down by someone playing devil's advocate for their own selfish reasons. I've seen it happen repeatedly, primarily in meetings, and at the huge cost of company time and money. Still, if you're aware of and prepared for this sort of response from Negative Nate, it's not impossible to defuse the situation. Steal his thunder. Start out by identifying the negatives: "I realize that by implementing the new policy, we're opening the window for problems A, B, and C; however..." and go on to emphasize the positive elements of the proposal.

Are *you* the negative person? Not sure? Ask. Ask people who will tell you the truth, not the people who will fill it with fluff and not want to hurt your feelings. Then figure out what is causing you to be negative. Is it a current relationship? Is it your job? Your company? Figure it out and make the appropriate change. Life is too short to go through it seeing and feeling only the negative side of things. We have all been dealt some tough cards. Take some time to find the positive in your life.

Think of ways in which you can turn your less than positive attitude around. Do you like music? Play it constantly. Put family pictures in your car, at your desk, in your wallet. Cut out funny cartoons and put them on the refrigerator. Call a friend who is positive and talk with them. You can decide today that you are going to work toward a more positive attitude. The choice is yours.

How do you avoid hiring negative people? By asking the right questions? How about "What drives you nuts about customers?" "Give me the last time you had a negative experience with a clerk (or whatever)."

Do not let negativity take over your workplace. Do not let it control your life.

It's All About the Attitude—and the Passion

There have been entire books written about attitude. Entire books because attitude is everything. I always tell managers "bad attitudes begin at the top." Oh, they get so mad at me. But, it's true. If a manager has a bad attitude, then what else can he expect from the rest of the staff? If the manager has an *outstanding* attitude, he won't tolerate the negativity for very long.

"Excellence is not a skill. It is an attitude."
~ Ralph Marston ~

I often associate attitude with passion. When I applied for the Executive Director's position at the Troy Chamber of

Commerce in 2000, I didn't think I had a chance. We had just moved to the area two months prior and people told me "that job is who you know." We certainly didn't know many people yet, especially the power dogs, but I sent my information in anyway. In just two weeks I was called for an interview. I took my portfolio with me, containing my resume, cover letter, reference letters, job samples, honors, and my very best attitude.

I had researched the Troy Chamber, as well as many other Chambers, drawing comparisons and outlining differences. I brought along with me fifteen ideas I thought the Chamber might consider incorporating or at least looking into. For example, the Chamber had 111 members but there were over 300 potential members in Troy alone, not even including any of the surrounding areas. I had ideas on membership recruitment, retention, and much more. While they reviewed the information, I explained that even if I did not receive the job that they were welcome to keep the information for the person who was chosen for the position.

The group of six asked the usual questions: "Why are you leaving your current job," and I answered, "I need something more fulfilling. I would like to find an organization that is looking for someone who is interested in a career in the industry." As the interview came to a close, the chairperson said "we will contact you to let you know if we will be scheduling a second interview." One member of the panel said, "Wait a minute. This girl has passion, and that is what we need in this job. She is not going to be afraid to take risks and take this organization in a direction that it needs to go. I would like to hear more." So, I stayed another fifteen minutes answering questions.

During the second interview, the panel brought with them the list of ideas that I had originally submitted. They noted that they were quite impressed by my initiative and asked me if this was a one-time thing or if it was something I could continue to do. At that point, I pulled out another list of ideas, generated by doing more research and simply looking around the community for opportunities...what was, what wasn't, what could be. I got the job.

I tell you that story because they did not hire me for my skills alone; they hired me because I had passion. You cannot train passion. It comes from inside. And it can wear as many definitions as the number of people attempting to describe it. But in simplest form it's the strength of emotion and belief that generates the drive and energy in attaining your goal. Do what you love, and the passion will be there.

Things to consider:

How do you find those potential employees who have passion?

Many times people with passion have friends with passion.

Also remember that positive attitudes start at the top.

Choosing Your Attitude is All Up to You

> *"The trick is in what one emphasizes. We either make ourselves miserable, or we make ourselves happy. The amount of work is the same.*
> ~ Carlos Castaneda ~

Bad attitudes. I hate them. Yes, I know, I have *had* them--but I still hate them. What can you do to change your attitude? First and foremost, decide your attitude before you get out of bed. I will readily admit that I am not a morning person, and when that alarm goes off at 6:00 a.m. I can assure you that it is not pretty. One morning I could not get the alarm to shut off, so I finally took my hand and gave it a solid whack. The alarm stopped, never to ring again. It might have been a defective product, or possibly had something to do with hitting the floor and breaking into small and unidentifiable pieces.

As I was shopping for a replacement alarm I thought to myself, "Wouldn't it be nice if I didn't have to wake up to that loud and annoying buzz?" So, I bought an alarm with music instead. Now every morning I am pulled from sleep by what I love most – music—melodies and words that start my day on the right foot before they even touch the floor. I'm still not a morning person, but that annoying alarm is a thing of the past; and my attitude is given a gentle nudge in the right direction before I'm even out of bed.

Your attitude can change any time you let it. Have you ever spilled your drink in your car and said, "Well, it is going to be one of those days." If you say it, then it will be. Or, you are running late and you get behind someone who is taking their own sweet time. What do you do? You get mad. Your blood pressure goes up. You arrive at work and tell everyone about your bad experience behind the wheel. (By the way, my mom says that you should have left the house earlier.)

If this happens to me, I can tell you what I do. I turn up the radio. First of all, is there anything that I can do about the speed of the car in front of me? No. Is this situation in my control? No. So, instead of sitting there and helping my blood pressure spike, I turn up the tunes. Try it.

For me, music is the answer in many situations. If I am traveling for training or a presentation and the chosen topic is "Attitude Adjustment," I'm jamming to some rock and roll as

I'm headed down the interstate. If I need to wind down *after* training, I tune in to easy listening.

But besides music, there are so many other things that can immediately change your attitude. Think about your children, your grandchildren. Think about your pets. I have a picture of my husband on my desk, and on *good* husband days, that picture remains standing up. On *bad* husband days, I simply turn the picture face down on my desk. It's a little kooky, and I take good-hearted teasing about my mood barometer, but it works. Think about your last fun vacation. Pray. Go for a short walk. Do whatever it takes to refocus. We all have bad days and bad moments. That's only human. Just recognize them for what they are and be prepared for them— and the more prepared you are, the better

> "The most successful people
> are those who are good at plan B."
> ~ James Yorke ~

Or you can think of some jokes. *A mushroom walked into a bar and sat down. The bartender said, "I'm sorry, we don't serve mushrooms." And the mushroom said, "Why not, I'm a fungi."* A colleague of mine (who admits to having a bizarre sense of humor) recently found what she thought to be a great two-liner on the internet while doing some serious quote research for a business project. It kept her smiling for days whenever it crossed her mind: *Last night I played a blank tape at full blast. The mime next door went nuts.* Or we have my favorite Frisbee joke. *"I was wondering why the Frisbee kept getting bigger -- and then it hit me."* Whoa. Those are some winners. Okay, maybe I won't quit my day job for standup, but thinking about those jokes can sure change my attitude.

A past co-worker of mine has been a single parent for 16 years, and I've seen her struggle through some bad days, some bad years. Along the way she discovered that she had developed an accidental mantra of "it's only like this for right now"—and even when the "it" seemed to multiply and the "right now" felt like it lasted for two forevers, the positive attitude of getting beyond the rough spots kept her going. She's still going. And she's doing just fine.

In the business world, a positive attitude starts at the top. At one of my seminars I was introduced to a potential client who asked that I meet with him to discuss the possibility of conducting attitude training for his staff. He said he just couldn't figure out why everyone was so negative. He had high absenteeism among his employees, tardiness problems, and a huge turnover. So I scheduled an appointment with him.

I arrived at the office at 12:45 p.m. for a 1:00 p.m. appointment. He was late. Not only that, but he didn't apologize. He was rude to someone on the phone yet continued to talk for fifteen minutes about his "incompetent" staff. So, there I sat. What would I need to do in this situation? He said, "I want to hire you to fix those people out there." I said, "Well, let's see about scheduling training. When would you be available to participate?" He said, "I will not be participating. You need to fix *them*."

At that point, I realized he had no idea that he was the problem, or at least a large part of it. I took a breath and I went there. Yes I did. At this point I felt like there was no getting around it. I said, "Tell me about your attitude." He paused and said "What do you mean? My attitude is fine."

I began to tell him a story about a previous boss I had. I worked for a company for a long time, and after several years a new manager was hired. She was arrogant, self-serving, demanding, and it was her way or the highway. I noticed one day, during a conversation with a customer, that I sounded just like her. I stopped dead in my tracks. Never before had I realized that I tend to mimic my superiors. I could see the look on his face; and at this point, I wasn't sure what would happen. He ended our meeting rather abruptly, thanked me for coming in, and I went home.

Two days later I received the following e-mail: "I get it. I absolutely get it. I am the leader and as a leader I am also a mentor. If I want my staff to change then I need to change. When can you start?" It was a risk I took. But frankly, I wouldn't have accepted the job if he had refused to participate. Good or bad, problem or solution, managers must be involved.

Do you need an attitude check?

Notes

Notes

Chapter Five

We're All in This Together

"Bite off more than you can chew, then chew it."
~ Ella Williams ~

Above and Beyond

It's tough to get service "above and beyond" but I know it's out there. I've seen it, I've received it, and I've delivered it. But as much as twenty-five years ago the experts were touting that customer service was at an all-time low. If that's the case, and service began its nosedive in the eighties, what would those experts think of it now? And what caused it? More difficult yet, how do we fix it?

Each generation, each decade, prides its own name, its own unique label and defining philosophy; and over the years, as I've spoken to many people about this decline, I've repeatedly heard the consensus that the eighties wove the fabric of "looking out for number one." Books were written about it, song lyrics advised it—and we read, and we listened, and we sang along.

Maybe we needed that at the time. No one would argue that society is continually changing, and we have to change with it or get lost in the dust. The trick, as always, is to keep the best of what's salvageable from the *good old days* while adjusting to the new. Maybe we just threw too much away. The sixties were turbulent—in too many ways—and the seventies are remembered by some as having been a more gentle and healing decade. But then came the eighties, when the importance of "self" became paramount. Our egos were bolstered; and the positive slant to confidence, image, and self-esteem may have gotten a little out of kilter. Fanatically *looking out for number one* can totally unbalance the complementary elements of being other-directed and yet self-preserving... tipping the scales completely toward self-infused behavior.

But exemplary service still exists. There are days when it seems to have been kidnapped by the bad guys, or simply traveling incognito, but nevertheless I continue to find good examples, often when I need them most.

> ➢ We had stayed all night at a local hospital with my dad. I had been up all night with no food, no sleep, and my nerves were getting the best of me. Even with an empty stomach, my body was fighting against itself and I knew I was going to be sick. The brain can send out some really confusing signals at times. So I locked myself in the hospital bathroom and dealt with the nonsense and exhaustion of dry heaves. In the middle of all that, I heard a knock on the door. "Dawn, are you okay? Is there anything I can do for you?" It was my Dad's nurse. I said, "No thanks. I'll be out in a minute." When I was finally feeling better and came out of the restroom, there sat a cup of ice, a white soda,

some soda crackers, and my dad's nurse with a sympathetic smile on her face, saying, "I thought those might help your nerves."

➤ During another all-nighter with Dad at the hospital...the first morning I was there a lady walked in and asked me "coffee or tea?" I said, "No, my dad is on a restricted diet." She said, "No Ma'am, I meant for you." I thanked her for the offer and told her that I wasn't really a coffee or tea drinker—that I'd head down to the cafeteria shortly to get a Diet Pepsi. I was putting on my shoes and brushing my hair to go to the cafeteria when the door opened and there she stood, with a can of Diet Pepsi and a cup of ice. She said, "You looked pretty tired. We want to do everything we can to make your stay more pleasurable." (Remember, we are at a hospital, not a hotel.)

➤ I rarely see my regular doctor because it is so much easier to get in with his P.A. And who *wouldn't* want to see Dr. Dave. He walks in, shakes your hand, asks you how you are doing, and is honestly prepared to spend time with you. He makes it seem like he has all the time in the world, when in fact his patients are usually in and out in five minutes. It just doesn't feel that way. He asks about your overall health and asks if you have any questions or concerns. Then he addresses them. When *I'm* the patient, he always asks about my Mom. Like me with my high-powered Rolodex, he may just take great notes and have it written in my chart—but I don't care, he still remembers. And that's what matters.

➢ My mom took her brother to a Cancer Center in St. Louis. While her brother was getting a treatment, one of the center's personnel came up to her in the waiting room and said, "I can relieve some of that tension in your neck if you'd want me to." Mom said, "I'm sorry. I'm not the patient." The staff member smiled and said, "I know, but we know you're dealing with a lot of stress. It shows." She massaged her neck and truly took away some of the stress.

> *"Treat all customers as if they sign your paycheck*
> *...because they do."*
> ~ Anonymous ~

What is your company doing to go "above and beyond?" What *should* you be doing?

The Good, The Bad, (and the Ugly?)...All in the Same Place

We went to a very nice restaurant; we had a mediocre experience with the hostess (nothing too exciting), but oh were we surprised when our busser arrived. He said, "How is everything this evening? My name is Sam and I will be taking care of refilling your drinks; but if you need anything else just let me know. My goal is that you have a great experience while you are here." WOW, were we ready for a fantastic evening. Our waitress came and took our order (again, nothing too exciting) then back again came Sam. He smiled and asked,

"Can I get either of you anything?" Oh yeah. The busser definitely exceeded our expectations—of the *busser* anyway.

So, the next time we were deciding on a restaurant we chose this one again, in hopes of sitting at Sam's table. But as we were being seated we didn't see him. We asked and were told that it was Sam's night off. Our busser was approaching, and we were anticipating that he might meet or exceed Sam's level of service. The busser reached our table, turned over our glasses, poured our water, and walked away. No Sam. Not even close—and the rest of our night was a downer. Sam had set the benchmark for all others to meet or exceed and, no pun intended, no one else stepped up to the plate.

Product Knowledge

You read on the bank's marquee, "ask us about our CD specials." So, you go into the bank and ask the first person you see. They respond with, "Well, Bob is not here right now but he should be back around 3:00 p.m. He's the one who knows about the CDs." My point is that there is very basic company knowledge that every employee should have. Employees themselves should be responsible for keeping current on new information, just as it is management's responsibility to provide them with that product information. Too often an answer like the one above is just an easy excuse. The resources and answer are there but the staff is just not willing to find it. Product knowledge is everyone's responsibility.

I went to the local movie store to rent a movie. I am not much of a film buff, so when I do rent one I hope that it is something great. As I approached the counter, I asked the employee, "Have you ever seen this movie?" He said, "No, I don't even like movies". Well, okay then.

How well does your staff know your product?

The Importance of Follow-up

I was in the market for a new car, a task I absolutely despise, but it had to be done. My first thought was that I needed to drive around to different dealers to see what they had to offer. The first dealer provided me a salesperson who walked me around the lot and showroom, answered all of my questions, and acquired some of my very basic information (name, phone number, and e-mail address). He didn't have any of the cars that I liked in stock but he promised he would get back to me once he attained some additional information. Before I got home, I had an e-mail waiting for me, following through with what he'd promised and the information that I needed. Also, a few days later, he followed up with a phone call to see if I had made a decision or had any other questions.

The second dealer I went to was just as nice. We discussed some car options and he also took the same pertinent information as they had at dealer #1. Months later, I still have heard nothing back from him.

The third dealer I went to was also just as nice. We again discussed the various car options, he thanked me for coming in, and that was it. He has no opportunity to follow up with me because he doesn't have any information about me. Doesn't it seem as if they missed the boat here? Who do you think is going to get my business?

What kind of follow-up does your business have?

Upsell ~ It Really Helps the Bottom Line

Oh, such a missed opportunity. You know, it's the old "do you want fries with that?" But let's take it a step further—all the way to visualization. You are sitting at a restaurant and you just finished your meal when the waitress asks you if you would like dessert. You look at the rest of the party and everyone is as unsure as you are, or at least pretending to be. But if the waitress approaches your table with a dessert tray, displaying all the temptations as she asks if anyone would like dessert, the odds are in the restaurant's favor that at least one of you will order dessert. What an upsell.

What can your company upsell?

➤ An oil change business can offer a tire rotation
➤ A carpet cleaner can offer a deodorizer
➤ A veterinarian can offer tick prevention medicine
➤ An attorney can upsell a simple will
➤ A physician can upsell a cholesterol test
➤ A gym can upsell a personal training session
➤ A weight loss company can upsell a monthly pass
➤ A pharmacy can upsell multivitamins
➤ A dentist can upsell a teeth whitening
➤ A makeup counter can upsell makeup remover

The list is quite endless. Make a list of five things your company can upsell. If you get stuck and need some inspiration, take a look at past sales receipts.

Make it Personal

I love walking into my favorite restaurant and hearing them say, "Hey, Dawn!" That's exciting to me on so many levels. First because they took the time to learn and then remember my name; and better yet, they say it with a smile and make me feel that they are genuinely glad to see me.

I was totally impressed one time when the waitresses came to my table and handed me a newspaper article. She said that she knew I was interested in service and wanted to show me the article, one that spoke of the need for improvement in the service industry. She gets it.

In my business I meet a lot of people. So, you can imagine that as I shop for groceries or walk around the park, I will invariably run into someone who was in one of my training sessions. Many times I can place them, but usually they will say "I saw you when you trained at ____. My name is ____ and I really enjoyed your seminar." I always take the time to speak with them; and when I get home I look up their company address and send them a card. This tells them that not only did I enjoy speaking with them, but that I appreciated their taking the time to stop and talk with me. Those individuals remain customers forever.

What ideas do you have to make it personal?

- ➢ Take your clients some cookies or doughnuts—just because. Enclose a card that says, "Thank you for being our client. Enjoy!"
- ➢ Know your clients' names and expect your staff to learn their names as well.
- ➢ Invite your clients to lunch and ask them how your company can better assist them. You could hear some great ideas and get an excellent

perspective from someone who is utilizing your business.

Think about other ideas with a personal touch, and then put them into play. The results will be dramatic.

Meeting Personal and Practical Needs

Have you ever had blood drawn? It's not exactly something we spend time thinking about, or get excited about—just one of those things that sometimes needs to be done. So, is it enough for the person to simply draw the blood?

Let's consider this scenario. You sit in a room, the phlebotomist arrives, he ties your arm with a band, finds your vein, wipes your arm, inserts the needle, draws the blood, pulls out the needle, puts a cotton swab and band aid on it, folds your arm, and then leaves the room. Was your practical need met (drawing the blood)? Yes. What about your personal need? Of course not. Heck, the person didn't even open his mouth. Now let's look at the way that it should have happened.

➤ Phlebotomist should have knocked on the door and addressed you by name.

➤ He should have smiled, shaken your hand and introduced himself.

➤ If appropriate, he should have sat next to you and gone over your chart and the procedure to be done.

➤ He should ask to take your hand in order to see your vein.

➤ At this point, the conversation should serve to direct the patient through the rest of the process.

> ➤ Once the blood is being drawn, he should not miss the opportunity to make casual conversation—talk of local news, weather, things you may have in common, etc. This helps distract the patient and pass the time. If it is apparent that the patient does not wish to talk, that's okay. At least an effort has been made to personalize the situation.
> ➤ Once completed with the task, he should thank the person for coming in and let them know where they should wait, making certain to include the next step in the process.
> ➤ His last comments should be "is there anything else I can do for you" and "have a nice day." What a difference. It's day vs. night.

What do you need to do to meet both the personal and practical needs of your customer?

Going the Extra Step

"There are no traffic jams along the extra mile."
~ Roger Staubach ~

No traffic jams? Well, that's kind of sad. You'd think any smart business person would be out there fighting for the lead, elbowing his way through the crowd of *other* smart businesses to be the very best in the eyes of the customers. At times it's an easy enough job to identify areas for improvement, but knowing and saying doesn't always translate to doing. You have to walk the talk. And it truly is only a *walk*, not a marathon run.

Smart companies seem to be shifting focus from product-centered to customer-centered operational policies—knowing that pumped-up customer service can bring a greater degree of success and profit than attempting to increase business through the lure of discounted pricing. In the long run, it costs more to attract new customers than it does to retain established ones. But you want and need them both. It's simple human nature that people want to be treated well; and when your customers realize that they're receiving enhanced service, you're paying attention to the small details and actually taking the time to see them as a person and not a number, they're going to stay put.

Realtors know that a bad first impression with a potential buyer can ruin the chance of selling the house. How can a realtor go the extra step?

➤ Serve cookies and punch at an open house—or match the refreshment to the style of home that's being toured...a champagne or sparkling cider reception for a $4 million home, more casual fare for a cozy home

➤ Have a give-away for the potential buyers (i.e. a can coolie, a magnet with a schedule of the local sports team, etc.)

➤ Make sure the house smells great (candles or other fragrance sources, maybe with the scent of fresh cookies, apples, cinnamon, vanilla...)

There should also be a registration sheet for all who attend the open house. A handwritten note to the potential buyers will *wow* them; it should thank them for touring the house and let them know that the realtor will be more than happy to keep an eye out for their ideal home.

Do you utilize every opportunity to acquire a database of your clients? A great way to obtain the information is to have a drawing in which they provide their address. Or you may choose to offer e-mail coupons and ask for e-mail addresses. If you own a restaurant, you can develop a birthday registry book; and after learning the person's birthdate, you can mail them a discount coupon to be used for their birthday dinner at your restaurant. It may be a great incentive as they make the decision of where to spend their birthday. It is also likely they will not be dining alone on such a special day, so the additional business you've gained can grow exponentially with very little effort. Going still another extra mile, offer them a coupon as they leave—another discount to be redeemed if they return within a month or two.

What if you see one of your customer's pictures in the newspaper? What if their daughter is getting married? Want to "wow" them? Cut out the picture, laminate it, and mail it to them with a handwritten note. Who else is going through this much trouble? Thankfully, not many. You want to stand out and you want to care.

Go that extra step for your staff and your customers, every single day. At my mom and sister's bar, birthdays are celebrated in style. But instead of the ubiquitous birthday cake and candles, they serve a large beef stick crowned with a lighted birthday candle. As offbeat as it sounds, you'd have to agree that it's much better bar food than cake and ice cream. The unique presentation has become a talked-about tradition, and it has customers returning time after time and bringing their friends.

"Here is a simple but powerful rule - always give people more than what they expect to get."
~ Nelson Boswell ~

Taking Orders

Good waiters and waitresses "get it." They fill up your drinks (even if you are not their customer), they wait the appropriate time to check on you, and they clear your plates properly and politely. But often times we see one small problem. When they take your order, they are concerned only about getting through the process. Here's an example:

"I'm Cindy and I'm here to take your order. Sir, what will you have?"

"I'll have a steak with..."

"How would you like that steak?"

"Medium. With that steak I would like the vegetables and..."

"How would you like the vegetables cooked?"

"Grilled. Also, could I have ..."

And so on.

Some waiters/waitresses try to solve this problem by taking the lead.

"I'm Cindy and I'm here to take your order. Sir, what will you have?"

"I'll have a steak with vegetables."

"And how would you like your steak prepared, sir?"

"Medium would be fine"

"We would also like to cook the vegetables to your specifications. Do you have a preference?

Sometimes people operate like robots. Do you really want your staff just going through the motions like automatons?

Give Them More Than They Expect

We recently took a balloon ride, a gift from my husband for our anniversary in May. Due to weather and schedule conflicts, we did not take the balloon ride until October; but as it turned out, we picked the best weekend when the fall leaves were at the height of their color.

The balloon ride was listed on my "Top 25 Things to Do before I Die" list, and I had envisioned the ride in my head for many years. We would be floating in the air, above the earth, and seeing and feeling things that we never had before. So, going into this experience I had my expectations well set.

We arrived at the pick-up location, and it was immediately obvious that several balloons were going out that day. We weren't greeted by anyone so we located someone who looked like they worked for the company. We asked for the owner and were told that he hadn't arrived yet, so we sat in limbo and waited until he made an appearance. Once he got there, we all were asked to review our paperwork with him (and basically sign our lives away – ha-ha). He introduced us to our balloon captain and our balloon follower after which we were loaded into his personal truck. Clearly he had not taken the time to clean out the truck—there was quite a lot of trash and the carpets hadn't been vacuumed in years. He also noted that one of the seat belt clips was broken but assured us that if we pushed hard enough we could get it to work.

We pulled away and began our journey to the lift-off site. Ted and I were in the back seat and they were in the front seat. The front seat group talked amongst themselves about things that were going on in their lives; and after a while the balloonist asked if we had ever been up in a balloon before.

We said "No." He explained how the balloon would take off, how it would land, things to expect, etc.

We arrived at the lift-off destination and they rolled the balloon out. They involved us in holding ropes, opening the balloon, and a lot of the basic pre-flight needs. And before we knew it, we were off. He had brought two waters for each of us. The view was incredible—everything that I had expected. (Did I mention that I am afraid of heights? My thought—my hope—was that this would help me with that. And it did.) He explained, here and there, where we were, special buildings, highways and other landmarks.

After our hour was up, we landed at a high school. Everyone assisted in putting the balloon back in the trailer and we drove back to the start location. As we were driving, the two began their own conversation again. The balloon follower said "I don't understand where Illinois drivers learned to drive. I was even out in Arizona and got behind a driver that clearly hadn't been to driving school. Guess where they were from? Yep, Illinois." He then turned slightly and said, "I hope you folks aren't from Illinois." Yep, we are.

After we arrived at our car the owner had a champagne celebration, with imprinted wine glasses (that we kept), a certificate of completion, and a short speech.

Overall the experience was fun. Would I do it again? Probably. But, what I thought about afterward was all of the missed opportunities there had been to exceed my expectations. Here are some thoughts:

➢ Get us involved in the conversation and use the drive to "pump us up" for the ride. Talk about the past great experiences.

➢ Do a little homework. There was a ton of paper-work to fill out that we had to mail in. How about adding a question like "what is your favorite non-alcoholic beverage?" or "Have either of you ever been in a balloon before?" Doing your homework will help you build a relationship with that customer.

➢ Take our picture in the balloon and send it to us. (We had a camera but we had to take off so fast we could not have taken the picture. Our balloon follower could have used his camera, but he didn't.)

➢ Find out if we just want to enjoy the balloon ride quietly (with little talk) or if we would like to hear specifics about what is below.

➢ Follow up with a thank you note, some cards to give our friends, and a survey to find out how they did.

Watch details like dirty cars, first impressions, etc. All of your competitors are doing the same fundamental things as you. What are you doing to EXCEED your customers' expecta-tions?

To the Point of No Return

"If we don't take care of our customers, someone else will."
~ Anonymous ~

Sometimes people just leave dissatisfied. The trick is to find out why they are dissatisfied, *before* they leave. Not as easy as it sounds. The difficulty lies simply in the fact that in many cases it creates an uncomfortable situation, and no one enjoys a potential confrontation with a customer. More times than not statistics are on your side, suggesting that if you can rectify a situation sincerely and immediately, that 95% of the customers will return.

So, be brave. Step one: you ask them and they tell you. Step two: you must thank them for their candor, try to remedy whatever dissatisfied them, and do what you can to get them back in the door for a second chance. How do you do that? Well, it depends on what displeased them.

If they were dissatisfied about the level of service, you must determine what it was. Did it take too long to get acknowledged? Were their expectations not met? Was the service level lacking or not to their satisfaction?

Take a moment to write down the top ten reasons people may not return. Now imagine that they're standing face to face with you, explaining their dissatisfaction. What would you say to them? Here are some things to think about:

My steak was not done properly.

> *Your first thought could be: "Well how did you order it?"*
>
> *Answer should be: "I'm sorry that your steak was not cooked to your order. How would you like it prepared—I'll ask the chef to prepare another and we'll bring it out as soon as possible.*

The receptionist made me wait ten minutes before she called you to tell you that I was here.

First thought could be: "Maybe she was busy."
Answer should be: "I apologize for your wait. You have my undivided attention right now."

I couldn't find a place to park.

First thought could be: "So?"
Answer should be: "I am sorry that all of the parking spaces were taken. We are so proud that our business has grown but we will definitely look into the parking situation. Thank you for letting us know."

You did not clean this suit the way I asked.

First thought could be: "We cleaned it."
Answer should be: "I am sorry. If you have a special request we will make it a first priority. Thank you for letting us know."

Your restroom was filthy.

First thought could be: "No it's not!"
Answer should be: "I am sorry if there's been a problem. We will have someone check them immediately. Thank you for letting us know."

The person who registered me was a robot.

First thought could be: "She registers fifty people a day."
Answer should be: "I am sorry. Our goal is to process people as quickly as possible so that they don't experience a long wait; but at the same time, we try to take enough time with

them and treat them as individuals. Thank you for letting us know."

I didn't like your employee's tone of voice with me.

First thought could be: "How was your tone of voice with them?"

Answer should be: "I apologize for any communication that seemed inappropriate. I will speak with the employee. Thank you for letting us know."

The checker never said a word to me.

First thought could be: "Did you talk with them?"

Answer should be: "I am sorry about your experience with our checker. Our goal is to process the customers through as quickly as possible, still allowing time to speak with them. Thank you for letting us know."

I didn't know you closed at ten because your hours aren't posted anywhere.

First thought could be: "Duh. We close at 10:00."

Answer should be: "I apologize for the inconvenience. We will be posting a sign to avoid future confusion. Thank you for letting us know."

"You cannot always control circumstances, but you can control your own thoughts."
~ Charles Popplestown ~

Once you get through thinking about possible answers, figure out what your next step would be. For example, if someone said "Your restroom is filthy." Your first thought should not be "It is not." You should take a good look at the restroom and see where they are coming from.

As a secret shopper, I can discover things that people had no idea were wrong. Many times the dirty restroom comes up. I hear managers say "so, we aren't a restaurant, we're a bank. There is no trash on the floor." No, there is no trash—but take a better look at the ceiling vents, or the top of the stall. There are usually layers of dust. The point is that businesses who want to exceed customer expectations should pay attention to detail.

Instead of being defensive in the face of your customer's comments, embrace them. Otherwise there is no sense in asking for constructive feedback. If you prefer a less personal method to obtain feedback, it can be acquired via survey; but remember that these are not quite as effective as one-on-one. A survey needs to be brief with both open and closed-end questions. Important questions to include:

➢ Will you return? Why or why not?
➢ Was your overall experience positive, negative or mediocre?
➢ Will you tell your friends about your experience? Why or why not?
➢ What one thing could we do next time to take your experience over the top?

The questions should be very specific and the questionnaire should be kept short and sweet. The questionnaire should be mailable (with prepaid return postage) or a box for their collection should be placed where everyone has easy access. (It should also be locked, so employees cannot go digging through it to throw out the bad ones.)

So, you get the questionnaires back. Now what do you do? Keep a database of answers, focusing on the needs for improvement. Work with your staff on an improvement process. Let's say that "too long of a wait" is the suggestion most often noted. What could you do? The first thing you should look at is the actual wait time. In some cases it's just an issue of misperception, but when there is an excessive wait time, how can that be reduced? After you have addressed that issue, you should take a look at how you can facilitate the wait. Not quite sure how to do that? Both you and your staff should go to the waiting area and just sit there. What might help the time pass more quickly?

The goal is for the customer to return.

Why Do People Not Return?

> "Do what you do so well that they will
> want to see it again and bring their friends."
> ~ Walt Disney ~

Well, there are many reasons. But adding the research that I have done to personal experience, the equation to determine failed customer retention usually equals poor service. Think of the last time you decided not to return to a business. Did it have something to do with the service? What would it take for them to regain your business? Once you have had poor service, it is hard to forget about it. Remember, 90% of the people who have received poor service never explain why they do not return. They just disappear.

Why do people not tell the company why they choose to take their business to a competitor? Do you? Here is my question – if people are not returning to your company for their repeat business, why not ask the reason? Are you afraid of what they might say? Well, instead of being afraid, embrace it.

If someone says to you "the reason I do not return to your business is because of the lack of parking," if you hadn't heard it directly from them, you might never know. Wouldn't it be great for customers to step right up and offer their reasons for choosing not to return? How would you take that advice? It's often hard to take constructive criticism. By dealing with each situation individually, you can possibly save that customer from leaving.

"Customer complaints are the schoolbooks
from which we learn."
~ Anonymous ~

There are countless reasons why I have not returned to businesses. One example happened many years ago in a jewelry store. I always make it a point to support small businesses whenever possible and decided to make a planned purchase at a local jewelry store rather than a large franchised operation. I entered the store, a small but empty showroom where no one greeted me. After several minutes, an employee finally emerged from the back room. I could hear the television playing and it sounded like a commercial had come on. She asked if she could help me. I said, "I am looking for a heart necklace," and she showed me the case where they were displayed. It was then that the phone rang; and from the tone of voice and conversation it was obviously a personal friend. I heard that her daughter had a problem with a teacher, that she had forgotten to take the hamburger out of the freezer, and the fact that oh-how-she-wished that she wasn't at work. At the end of her phone conversation, she returned to the back room. (I'm not sure why—maybe to try to catch a few more minutes of her soap). When she returned after a short time she asked, "Have you made a decision?" I smiled and said, "yes" and turned around and left the store.

The worst part of the whole story is that the owner didn't know why I never returned. But, guess what? As coincidence would have it, I was conducting a seminar a couple of months later and...you guessed it. The owner was in my class. She came up and introduced herself to me. She asked if I had ever been in her store and without hesitation, I told her the story. She explained that over the summer she brings in college students to "watch her store" while she goes on vacation. I guess the students "watch people come in and watch people leave" without making a purchase and without receiving good service. Surprisingly, she didn't seem shocked or concerned over the incident. But things may change when she reads this book.

Is there a reason why we don't ask them why they don't return? Yes, because the truth hurts. What if someone was very honest with you and said, "I don't return because of the poor service you gave me last time." Well, you could be defensive or pout in the corner, but what would the correct reaction be? To accept the constructive criticism and learn from it? Good answer. Give yourself an A+...the A for correctness, the + for bravery.

Do you have 100% retention? Why do people not return to your business? Develop ways of finding out. The most forthright approach would be to candidly ask them--then take their information and run with it. Be open and make improvements as needed. Consider every single suggestion.

Notes

Chapter Six

You, Me, and the Other Guy

*"There is only one boss. The customer.
And he can fire everybody in the company
from the chairman on down,
simply by spending his money somewhere else."*
~ Sam Walton ~

Be Aware of Special Needs

Every customer is an individual--and each individual has special needs. Those companies that want to be great find a way to accommodate those needs in every way. At a senior citizen health day, the sponsor provided transportation from the car to the auditorium. It might not sound like a big deal to you and me, but to the seniors it was a gracious awareness of their decreased mobility and a guarantee that they wouldn't be worn out by the walk by the time they arrived at the auditorium.

A colleague of mine worked for many years as the event director at a private club. She often said that every time the phone rang she had a new boss. She wasn't even remotely complaining—she was simply allowing a normally unspoken perspective on the facts. Every customer is at least one-part employer...without customers you wouldn't have a job. She further described her position, and the necessity in remaining flexible in how she approached it, as *changing dance partners*. You may know the basic steps, but everyone has a different style; so when you change partners, you need to follow their lead.

Does your company cater to children, or do children often accompany their parents who frequent your business? What special needs do children have? A shorter drinking fountain. A changing table in the bathroom. A play area to keep them happy and occupied. Chairs that fit *their* size, not a grownup's. Look at ways that your company can better accommodate children.

How about certain adults? A larger-print menu. Assistance getting out of the car. What special needs do your customers have? How can you best accommodate them?

Make a list of customers' specific needs and share them with your staff.

Building Relationships Should be Top Priority

People who really want your business take the time to get to know you. I used to frequent a dry cleaner whose staff greeted me with, "Hey, Dawn, how are you today?" each and every time I walked in the door. They knew how I liked my husband's shirts starched. They knew that I was never in a rush to get my clothes. I continued to go there because *they just knew*. So, when their family business closed due to retirement, I was in shock. And I could only think "where will I go now where *they just know*?" I am still trying to find a place.

Do you utilize a particular business because of who you know? Then both of you have worked toward building a relationship; and that relationship itself allows a bit more room for errors. For example, let's use the same dry cleaner. I had been going there for years and years. Let's say on one visit they missed cleaning a spot. Because I had built that relationship, I would assume it was an oversight and move on. It just allows for some level of error.

But building relationships takes time, and where would I find the time? You just do. You use every opportunity to meet people, ask them questions (you cannot learn anything from speaking—you need to be listening) and getting to know them. I have found in my life that relationships that I make will find me forever.

Work for the People

For many years, my dad played with a band, and each weekend they performed to a crowded house. There was never a night without people requesting a special song, maybe the chicken dance or a circle dance. The band could have easily, and often happily, said, "No"—but why? That is what the people wanted. So they played the chicken dance and the circle dance, each time with enthusiasm, as if it were the first time and they were excited to play it. (Believe me, the chicken dance was *not* their song of choice.) Of course, the band had their favorite songs; and those always took second place to a customer's request. But the one thing I learned was that the band understood *who* they were playing for—they were playing for the crowd. If they ever forgot that, then it would be time to quit.

How many times do you think that Barry Manilow has performed the song "Mandy?" A few thousand times? Ten thousand times? Despite the numbers, if you attend one of his concerts you will think you are hearing it for the first time. Why? Because he knows that you are there to hear him sing, hear those fan favorites, songs that he's known and remembered for—and he strives each and every time to give it his best. If I went to a Barry concert (and I have been to each and every one in my area and even once in Las Vegas) and didn't hear "Mandy," it would be a huge disappointment; and I would leave thinking that he had sung only to please himself, without any concern for those fans who had been with him for so many years. Thank you, Barry, for making it right, each and every time.

⁂

Before I speak to a group, I always meet with the host to go over expectations and specifics of the event. I remember one client who expressly asked that no role plays, demonstrations, or audience participation be part of the speech. Wow! What a change from what I am accustomed to. I always realize who my customer is and my goal is to exceed their expectations. Had I not sat down with her to determine expectations, I would have failed—miserably. The event went off without a hitch and, in fact, I received a standing ovation. She was right. The crowd was not the type who would have enjoyed themselves had they been asked to be involved in active participation. And thanks to the opportunity to speak with her—really listen to her and then follow through—I had the benefit to know the audience as well. It was a win for both of us. For all of us.

What are you doing to work for the people? Do you know what your customers want? Do you know how to exceed those same customer expectations? If you are not positive of their expectations, simply ask them.

"Wowing" the Current Customer

We all have them—the customers who don't wait until the last minute to place their orders, or the customers who always pay their bills on time. Unfortunately, we spend 90% of our time with the 10% that make up the problem customer category—the ones who wait too late. Now is the time to think about how we can thank those excellent customers.

Each year I like to do something for each and every customer for whom I have done business. Many people send Christmas cards but I wanted to do something different. So, each August I take a night out to bake cookies and hand-write a thank you card. Why August? If I did it in December when everyone else did, I would get lost in the shuffle. But in August I am most likely the only one sending them a gift of cookies. And who doesn't enjoy cookies? Maybe even more so in summer, when they haven't already devoured every chewy, crunchy, flavor that can be imagined.

Most likely I have fewer clients than you, but think of something special that you can do for your clients. Are hand-written notes always out of the question? Let's say you have one hundred clients and three staff (including yourself). If each staff member wrote ten cards each day (taking approximately two minutes per card), you would be finished in only four days. The card should include a special mention about the person/staff.

Another idea might be to have a "Customer Appreciation Day". Invite the customers, their family, serve hot dogs, hire a clown, etc. It is a great way to meet their families and build a tighter relationship. Others will see how well you treat your customers and will want to be one of them.

What about sending a personal, handwritten card to a new customer within a week of their arrival? Whatever you can do to "WOW" them is something above and beyond what your competitor is doing.

> *"It takes less effort to keep an old customer
> satisfied than to get a new customer interested."*
> ~ Anonymous ~

Be Good, Be Great, or Be the Greatest – It's Your Choice

You must decide what makes your business a better choice than other businesses. Or what you can do to raise it to a higher level than that of your competition. Your business should stand out.

➢ Wipe the rain/snow from the carts
➢ Provide umbrellas (with your company name on them) or snow scrapers to customers on bad weather days
➢ Take a picture with your client in front of your company logo and send it to them (or in front of their new car or in front of an award they were part of helping you receive)
➢ Provide items that people continuously ask for (i.e. maps, phonebooks, notary service, pens, etc.)
➢ Send handwritten notes to visitors who sign your visitor book
➢ Give more than just a doggie bag—include extra sauce, dressing, bread, plastic ware...help

remind them of the positive experience when they sit down to eat the leftovers

- ➤ When bringing coffee, include condiments
- ➤ Wipe off the cup if it overflowed
- ➤ Sit down at a person's level when taking their order or speaking with them
- ➤ Always offer clients beverages and snacks
- ➤ Have each employee shake hands with the customers
- ➤ Scrape the windows of the customers' vehicles while they are doing business with you
- ➤ Send a handwritten note along with any completed paperwork
- ➤ Offer a to-go cup for their drink (if they are taking your cup with your logo on it, it's additional advertising for you)

The list is long. Please make it longer. What else can you add based on your own company and your personal brand of service? Have your staff share their input.

"You've got to look for a gap, where competitors in a market have grown lazy..."
~ Rupert Murdoch ~

But I Am Not on the Clock

I often see clients outside of the office, at grocery stores, in malls, at gas stations. I try my best to remember their names. But when I'm stumped, I don't let them see it—and I ask round-about questions until I figure out where I know them from and trigger the name in my memory. For example, "so how is business?" or "we have not seen you lately at any Business After Hours events" is usually enough to jog my memory.

⚜

So, I am in line at the grocery store, picking up only a few things, and trying to get out as quickly as I can. A client stops me to chit chat. What do I do? Well, I do what any good business owner would do, I chit chat. Now, I know what you are thinking. "What about getting out of the store quickly?" Well, I look at it this way. What would my client think? "She only wants to talk with me when it is convenient for *her*?" That doesn't make for good business.

A situation like this would also be a great time to get to know your client. Often, they have their children with them, or they are dressed casually and may be wearing a sport team shirt. Use the opportunity to your advantage. It's an unexpected chance to build a relationship with your client or further enhance the one that you have already established.

What else are you doing when you could be building a relationship? Is it more important than focusing on customer awareness? Imagine that you are at a bar having a drink after work, possibly waiting to meet business colleagues. But at the moment there is no one else in the bar except you and the bartender. He takes your order, serves up your drink, then walks away to wash dishes. An attempt was never even made to ask how you were doing. A good bartender will ask the right questions of his customers and determine if they wish to pursue a conversation.

"Small opportunities are often the beginning of great enterprises."
~ Demosthenes ~

Personalized Service Keeps Them Coming Back

I love getting a body massage, and I have been going to the same masseuse for many years. The trip to her studio is a little far to drive, but it's worth it. When I arrive, she is there—right there—in the moment. The ambiance is rich with lighted candles, fragranced pillows, a nice warm room, and some great massage music (she always asks what I would like to hear). Her soothing tone of voice and her skilled hands can do nothing but create the calm, serene feeling that I came for. When she is finished with the massage she always says, "thank you for the honor." Thank *me*? Let me thank *you*. I came in totally stressed and I leave feeling like a new person—and I'll be an even *better* new person as soon as my legs are no longer Jello® and my bones have somehow magically reconnected. But right now I'm loose and relaxed and feeling better than I have in weeks. Thank *you*.

As I left one day, I tried to understand what it was that helped to make me so calm—tried to dissect each element of the experience. Of course, the massage was the primary factor, but that wasn't all. The personalized service and attention to detail let me know that I was the most important person in her world, from the time I arrived, until the time I left. She plays the music I like (sometimes it is Barry Manilow and sometimes it is Carole King), and she remembers that I do not like the ocean sounds and other so-called massage music.

In preparing the room, she makes it special just for me. There are no dirty towels from previous customers or even the smallest remnant to indicate that anyone else ever uses that room, other than me. She creates the professional image that it is my room—all mine. When you call her to book a massage, she always says, with sincerity, "It will be nice to see you again." And once you arrive, your waiting time is zero (yes, zero) because she allows a fifteen-minute window between customers. When I asked her about that, she noted that she needed the time to transition from one customer to another. She had tried booking back to back but she felt rushed and was not giving the customers what they deserved and expected. She noted that she wants people to have time to get up after the massage, not have to rush getting dressed, have a relaxed drink of water before they go back out into the world. It's enough of a culture shock as it is—going from the quiet surroundings and feeling boneless to the noise and demands of the real world again.

Isn't she losing money? Couldn't she see one more client a day if she booked back to back? You know what she said? It is not about the money, it is about satisfying the customer, because when you satisfy the customer, the money will come. Oh yeah, she gets it.

With every positive experience it seems that you can always find a balance with a non-positive one. When my usual massage therapist was out of the country, I decided to try a more local person. Her building was only ten minutes from my home and the service was a savings of $15.00 per hour. When I arrived, I had to wait. The room was very dull, with nothing on the wall and nothing to read. When she finished with the appointment before mine she came out and said, "It will be a minute." When she was finally ready for me, she led me to a small room with four walls, a table, a jar of lotion, and nothing else. Yes, my back felt good when she was finished; but I realized at that point that going to get a massage is more than just having your back rubbed. I never went back to her studio.

✹

Linda at the local grocery store always greets me and mentions the weekly specials. "The whole chickens are $.79 a pound today if you were planning on chicken and dumplings," she says. How did she know I make chicken and dumplings? Because a few weeks earlier, as I was going through the checkout, she asked me what I was making for dinner and I told her. She was obviously paying attention. She was in the moment and focused on the customer. At the same time, she was also upselling this week's special and doing it quite successfully. I have yet to leave the store without picking up a special that she tells me about.

I have a friend who had to go to divorce court and, understandably, it was a very trying day for her. The following day she received a call from her attorney (not just someone on his staff, but her actual attorney)—he was calling to check on her. Now that is a perfect example of exceeding the customer's expectations.

How about my morning routine? Each day it was the same thing. I would stop for my soda and newspaper in the morning, get in line, pay for my items, and leave. This is the way it has been for years. Finally one day I decided to practice what I preach. I decided to find a place that appreciated my business, even if it was off the beaten path. I stopped in a small convenience store and, to my amazement, was actually acknowledged when I walked in. The friendly voice said "Good morning." My first thought was, "Good grief, are you really talking to me?" I poured my soda, picked up my newspaper, and took my place in line.

As I approached the counter as the next person in line, the friendly voice said, "Sorry about your wait. So how are you doing this lovely morning?" Wow! Customer service. I was in shock. I said, "I have to tell you that it's a pleasure to have someone with such a positive attitude in the morning." She said, "I believe it is all about the personal touch. If you treat people the way *you* want to be treated, they will come back."

She was right. If you treat people the way that you want to be treated, they *will* come back. And when they come back, they will spend money. This will lead to them telling their friends, and their friends will come to spend their money too—and when all that money isn't going to your competitors your business will profit. It is a big circle; and your positive attitude and personal service will keep it moving in your favor.

To me, the most important piece of customer service is consistency. It's important to remember that the first customer you serve in the morning and the last customer you serve at night all deserve the same excellent service. Think about this. If you worked for an amusement park at the information booth and the first person came in at 9 a.m. asking for directions to the restroom, you would put on your morning smile and say in your friendly professional voice, "Go past the Ferris wheel, make a right, and it is on your left." If the 42nd customer approached with the same question at 12:30 p.m., you would say in a somewhat friendly voice, "Go down to the Ferris wheel, make a right, and it is on your left." But by 4 p.m. it's hot, you're tired, your feet hurt, and it's been a long day. You are 15 minutes from clocking out. So that 157th customer approaches you asking for directions to the bathroom. You can't remember where you left your morning smile, your friendly professional voice has wilted to a hoarse croak, and it would be so much easier to snarl, "I've answered this question a thousand times today. It is down the street somewhere."

But if that's what happened, Mr. 157 would be more insulted than "amused" and would likely not make a return visit to your amusement park—at least not without some serious complaints to the management. Remember...what is the job of the information booth? They are established as a courtesy—*a courtesy*—to provide information in a friendly manner to each individual. The time of day has nothing to do with it.

What examples of personal service does your company have? What others could you add?

> *"When you start seeing your customers as interruptions, you're going to have problems."*
> ~ Kate Zabriskie ~

Know Your Customers—Their Wants and Their Needs

Most bowling alleys these days offer the additional service of children's birthday parties. But I would feel safe in assuming that few of them are choreographed by the super-hero who reigns at our local bowling alley. This particular birthday party coordinator is 60+ years of age, paid minimum wage, and the only paid hours she receives are those for the parties. Her duty sheet stated that she was to set up the children for bowling, bring out the drinks in the third frame, serve the pizza after the game, and bring the cake out a half hour later. She did all of that—and more.

The birthday boy was the first to arrive, and she had made certain that he would be thrilled with his party area. She had arrived at work early (but didn't clock in until her normal time) to decorate the birthday boy's chair with balloons, streamers, and a big Mylar balloon of a cartoon character.

The lanes were decorated with yellow and blue streamers and pictures of cartoon characters all over. Each child had a bowling ball waiting for them, along with a pair of bowling shoes.

As the guests arrived, they were greeted by the coordinator with a smile, a high five, and a token for the video games (to be used later). Once all of the guests arrived, she gathered them together and talked about bowling etiquette. She didn't say things like "don't walk on the lane with your regular shoes," "don't be talking to somebody when it is your turn to bowl," or "don't run up and down the aisles." She approached it in a completely different way. She said "Let's talk about how this particular cartoon character would bowl." She took her place on the lane and said, "On three, everybody cheer for your favorite cartoon character ... one, two --- three!" Everybody cheered for the cartoon character. She said, "Here is what the cartoon character would do. He would put on his bowling shoes, be ready for his turn, and hang with his friends. Can everybody do that?" They cheered again.

As each of the kids got up to bowl, she assisted when needed. She cheered them on, even when they didn't get a strike. She took pictures throughout the event. She brought the sodas to the table in the third frame and asked everyone to give a toast to the birthday boy. She included the parents in all of the fun, even offering to let them bowl on the next lane for free (upselling???). She brought the pizza when the bowling was over and guess what it was cut into – you guessed it, squares (just like that un-named cartoon character).

When it was time to open gifts, one really stood out among the usual bags and boxes. The birthday boy reached for the funny-shaped gift, opened it, and it was a brand new bowling pin. Everyone signed it and he was able to keep it as a souvenir.

The kids had all been given a token for the video games so she took them to the game room. As she walked with the kids she asked that the parents not clean up. They were to "kick up their feet and enjoy their free time."

As the kids began to leave, she thanked each of them for coming, again giving them a high five. She gave them each a pass to come back and bowl, and smiled to hear them telling their parents that they wanted to have their next birthday party there.

It's not over. Well, the party was over, but the experience wasn't. Two days later a card arrived at the home of the birthday boy. It read, "I hope you had a wonderful time at your birthday party. We were very happy that you chose our bowling alley to have fun with your friends. You will be able to remember your event for many years to come with the pictures that I have enclosed. Happy birthday."

Let's remember this – she made minimum wage. The bowling alley did not pay for the cartoon character stuff, the bowling pin wrapping paper, the card or the development of the pictures. She said it wasn't about the money at all. It was about creating an experience for the children.

> "A hundred years from now it will not matter
> what my bank account was, the sort of house I
> lived in, or the kind of car I drove...
> but the world may be different because
> I was important in the life of a child."
> ~ Forest E. Witcraft ~

The bowling alley has increased their birthday parties by 500% with word of mouth only. Sadly, the birthday party coordinator is still making minimum wage and to date, no one from the company has said "thank you" to her for all of her efforts. But, the children have some great memories to take with them.

Some people relate well to children and, well, I am not one of them. For whatever reason, it has never been my strength. Or at least not relating and dealing with groups of children. When I was very young and I first began looking for a job, my goal was to find something close where I could just walk and then eventually save up for a car. There was a day care just three blocks away and they were looking for a secretary. I went for an interview and was offered the job. I asked for an evening to think it over and as I was leaving, there was a screaming child and a frustrated Mom at the door. The screaming just curled my stomach. Thank goodness my gut feeling kicked in and I did not take the job. Although my secretarial skills were fine, I would have been no use to the employer. I would have dreaded going to work every day and everyone would have noticed it.

I try to talk with as many people as possible about service, staff, and really anything that they would like to talk about. I had a conversation with a lady who owned three local sandwich shops. She said "There is nobody in this town that really wants to work." I was a little taken back by the comment and I asked her what she meant. She said that she has hired over sixty people who have not worked out for her company in the last six months. She said "It costs me about $1,000 to hire an employee, and then after two weeks they quit." I asked her what qualifications she looked for when hiring people and she said, "Really, I'm looking for someone who has a decent attitude." Well, there you go. You hire decent and they remain decent.

I also asked her where she had been looking for new staff. She said she had been putting ads in the local newspapers. With that, you are only going to get people who read the local newspapers—which in itself is fine, but that should not be your only source. I told her to ask her top ten staff about people they knew to recommend. If they recommended someone who worked out and stayed for ninety days, that she would give them $100. She said, "$100?" I said, "Isn't paying someone $100 for a good employee better than losing $60,000 to bad employees?" She said, "Point well taken."

I also suggested that she go to the local high school and speak with a teacher who knows the best students. The best students are those who come to school every day, turn in their homework on time, have a positive attitude, etc. If the teacher recommends someone who stays for ninety days, offer them the same $100—to be donated to their classroom.

It is important to take a look at why people are leaving. The common denominator seems to be the manager (she didn't want to hear that). I asked, "What are you doing to retain good employees?" She said, "We give them a paycheck." Guess what? Everyone can give them a paycheck. You need to give them more. Here are some ideas:

➢ Thank your employees each day when they leave
➢ Offer incentives to everyone
➢ Recognize staff when they go above and beyond

Remember, it is rarely about the money.

Long-Standing Loyal Customers

We all have them: those customers who have been with us in both the good times and the not-so-good times. They have weathered the changes along with us and remained loyal through the growing pains of different staff, different products, and in some cases through different eras. What do you do for them?

Here are a couple of ideas from others:

A local coffee shop saw Alice and Greg every day. They were the most loyal customers you could ever find. Each morning both would order coffee and a pastry and enjoy the morning's newspaper. Alice and Greg also brought in new customers, as they mentioned and recommended the coffee shop to their friends. Attendance at the morning shop grew so much that the coffee shop had to expand.

One morning Alice and Greg arrived and the manager said, "We have something special for you." The manager had gone to the local dollar store and picked up a mug for each of them with their name on it. She said that now their most loyal customers have their own mugs. She thought Alice was going to cry. Heck, she thought *Greg* was going to cry. Alice and Greg continued to tell their friends about the mugs and soon there were even more loyal customers. So, the manager continued to find mugs with the loyal customer names on them. She called them the "Loyal Club Mugs." As people would walk in the door, their mug would be prepared with their drink of choice, and before they even reached the counter the mug was waiting for them.

One morning Greg arrived without Alice. He said that she was pretty sick and couldn't even get out of bed. So, after the shop closed, the manager packed up Alice's coffee mug, took Alice her favorite pastry and headed toward their house. Even though Alice wasn't up for coffee, they enjoyed their time together. Alice never forgot that.

Alice and Greg continue to go to their favorite coffee shop every morning, a shop that is now four times larger than originally. There have been four coffee shops in the area close because everyone wants to go somewhere that everyone knows them and where they have a mug with their name on it.

On one side of the issue, customer loyalty must be earned. On the flipside of that, it must be rewarded. How does customer loyalty begin? Through relationship building.
I have one particular place where I take my car for an oil change. Let me start with "I hate maintaining my car." So, choosing an oil change place is not on my top ten favorites list. But, I had heard from several people that they recommended this place so I decided to give them a try.

I drove up to the door and pulled my car in. The gentleman said, "My name is Rick and I promise to take care of you. How can we serve you today?" I said that I needed an oil change but that would be all for today. He said, "We are more than happy to help. I see that you have work laid out in your car. If it would be more convenient, you can stay in your car or you can feel free to go into our break room." I chose to stay in the car. He said, "No problem at all. Can I get you something to drink?" Something to drink? Wow! I declined but said, "thank you." At this point I realized that people had already been working on my car, draining out the old oil, checking my tires, etc. He said that he knew I was busy and that his goal was to get me through as quickly as possible.

I did some work and in what seemed like no time, Rick came to my window and said, "I think we are good. Could you please start your car and we can show you the oil line on the dipstick?" He said, "I know you said you just needed an oil change today so I will give you this printout to show you what your car manufacturer recommends. We hope you will consider us when you choose to do any other car maintenance."

He gave me his card and said, "We hope you come back and let some of your friends know about us. Here is a coupon for a free car wash. You can give this to Bobby at the car wash—it's good for a wash and a free vacuum too." Do you want to hear something strange? At that point I had no idea what I'd been charged for the oil change. But when I got home, I looked at the bill. It was the same price their competitor down the street was charging. For the same service? Not at all.

Yes, I told my friends and family and they all go there now. On my second visit to the oil change shop, as I pulled in the gentleman said, "Welcome back." And I thought, "How the heck did he remember me?" Well, they keep your license plate number in the computer and as you are pulling around, someone is entering it into the computer. They knew what type of oil I needed, that I liked to sit in my car, and they even said, "Thank you for referring your mom and your sister. They said you liked ice cream, so enjoy some on us at the dairy bar right down the street." Another WOW!

Now, here is my question, who couldn't be loyal to this organization? They get it. They really get it. There was so much going on here. There was cross-selling, the car wash, the dairy bar. Clearly they were listening to both my mom and my sister. I used to dread getting my oil changed but now, well, I never go over 3,000 miles...sometimes even sooner.

What loyal customers have you developed? We can never have enough of them.

Going Above and Beyond

My favorite indulgence is to get a pedicure. The other day I visited my favorite pedicure salon, and as I entered the salon the owner looked up and said, "Hi, Dawn" (name acknowledgement). On hearing my name, the other employees looked up and smiled (further acknowledgement). I took a seat and read the most current *People* magazine (keep up-to-date reading materials on hand). The chairs in the waiting room were comfortable (making the wait feel less) and clean (attention to detail-keep work and waiting area clean).

When they were ready for me, they came to get me (greeting me by name), took my purse and magazine for me (personal attention). They escorted me to the pedicure chair (very comfortable and modern), placing my personal items next to me (personal service). The chair -- let's talk about the chair. Remember, I am paying for a pedicure, but this salon invested in massage chairs that are to die for (going above and beyond). The roller rolls up and down your back and even heats up! It grabs your calves and massages them (oh yeah). As my pedicure began, they asked me to place my feet in the water, and then asked me if the water was the temperature I preferred. At that point, I think I was already too relaxed to answer.

Before beginning the pedicure, they make sure that all of their "tools" are within reaching distance (therefore, never leaving me alone.) Throughout the pedicure, they continue to ask me if everything is okay. Once the actual pedicure is complete, they move me to the waxing area (taking my belongings for me). The hot wax dip (also included in the price of the pedicure) is just another extra.

We are now at the end of our experience (that is what it is -- an experience). I pay, they thank me for coming (thank me for coming???) and off I go. I tell friends (referrals are your best marketing tools) what great service I receive, and it helps their business.

Does any of this sound familiar? Have you ever received services of this magnitude? Think about all of the service transactions you make over the course of a week. Do any match up to this? This is how every transaction should be completed but sadly, not many of them reach this level of service. I know I am going for a pedicure, to have my feet scrubbed and my toes painted, but really, it is the experience that I enjoy. You could have the best pedicure in the world but if the *service* is horrible, that's the part that you will remember.

> *"You have to perform at a consistently higher level than others. That's the mark of a true professional. Professionalism has nothing to do with getting paid for your services."*
> ~ Joe Paterno ~

A local florist has found a unique way to go above and beyond. Their delivery staff carry cameras to take a picture of the recipient with their arrangements. They then send the photo, along with the bill, to the person who placed the order. They also send a copy of the picture to the recipient with an enclosed card and list of arrangements offered. (They see this person as a potential customer. They have experienced the product firsthand.)

This is a small gesture but it accomplishes and paves the way for larger things. It gives the person who ordered the arrangement an idea of how the recipient felt and allows them to see exactly what they paid for. It also provides a further keepsake for the recipient while marketing the company to potential customer. The florist is the busiest one in the area and not necessarily the least expensive.

As always, it's those seemingly little things that count. We went to a restaurant and the waitress stooped down to take our order, equalizing the distance rather than towering above us. She addressed all of us with eye contact, even the children. She provided some fun stickers and coloring books for the kids. Later the manager came around, asking how things were, and offered to hang up the children's colored pictures for display. Nothing too major in any of that, but it made for memorable service.

What is your business doing to go above and beyond?

You Never Know

Have you seen the movie, *Pretty Woman*? My favorite part is when Vivian visits her first boutique. Because she doesn't have "the look", they assume that she doesn't have any money. Then later, she has an unlimited credit card and chooses to shop and *spend* at another boutique. After spending more than $10,000, and flaunting the shopping bags to prove it, she stops by the first boutique to show off the commission they "could" have earned.

Should you only treat customers nice when you earn a commission? Of course not. Your goal should be to treat every customer with respect.

A loan officer told me the story of a gentleman who came in off the street to compare loan rates. The customer entered the bank and asked to see a loan officer. Greg came out, shook the customer's hand, introduced himself, and asked the customer to come to his office. Greg offered him a refreshment and helped him off with his jacket, after which they spent about ten minutes discussing loan rates. Greg provided the customer with colorful brochures on a variety of items. The customer noted that he would take the items home to review them and compare the rates to the other financial institutions.

At the end of the conversation, Greg shook the customer's hand and thanked him for coming in. He walked the customer to the door and noticed that it was raining. Knowing that the customer did not have an umbrella, he asked him to wait a moment. Greg went back to his office for an umbrella. He escorted the man to his car under the umbrella, opened the door for him, and again thanked him for coming to their bank.

Just one week later the same customer came back just to see Greg. Greg noticed the customer in the lobby and immediately came out to greet him (by name). The customer asked Greg if he could meet with him briefly in his office. Once again Greg offered him a refreshment and helped him off with his jacket. The gentleman said, "Greg, I was so impressed with our last visit and how you really went above and beyond to assist me in every way. You did that, fully knowing you could not beat the loan rate I had at another bank, and for that, I would like to move all of my money to your bank." The customer handed Greg a bank book and asked him to open it. The gentleman had over one million dollars in four different types of accounts. The customer noted that "given the service you provided to a potential customer, I cannot wait to experience the level of service for current customers."

Guess what type of friends this customer has? You guessed it, rich ones. He sent everyone he knew to the bank to meet Greg. With that transaction and the referrals that followed, Greg won *employee of the year* at his bank. He brought in more new customers than any other employee at any of the bank's locations and all of that for some personalized service and an umbrella. We all know that every experience does not end like this, but still the possibilities are vast.

※

I was conducting a women's seminar for 200+ people. All of my seminars are very energetic, and to date no one has ever fallen asleep! For that I am grateful. After each event, I always take time to meet individually with people and answer any questions they might have. One lady approached me at the end of the seminar and asked what my recommendation was for a staff member with a bad attitude. I commented that I believe poor attitudes had much to do with poor management, whether that was hiring the wrong people or not setting a good example for the staff. She went on to say that many of her staff have poor attitudes and she was the PRESIDENT of the company! Oh man, I felt my face getting red. She shook my hand and said, "You have confirmed what I have been saying all along. I must project a positive attitude if I expect my staff to do the same because they are always watching." That person went on to become one of my biggest clients.

While in line at a department store, I noticed that the woman ahead of me was being treated with disrespect. The salesclerk made no eye contact and was answering the customer's questions with "yeah." When I approached the counter, the salesperson did a complete spin and treated me like gold. I couldn't figure it out—until another salesclerk approached and my salesclerk said, "Did you see who is here today? It is Mrs. Jones; she only comes in on sale days and wants her senior citizen discount each and every time." Say that again?

She is a recurring customer and we aren't treating HER with respect? Come to find out, Mrs. Jones was also the mother of a member of the store's Board of Directors. Hopefully she told her daughter about her experience.

Do you think you know everything about everyone who walks into your business? Absolutely not. But beginning today, you can find out.

Notes

Chapter Seven

Policies, Examples, and Stories, Oh My!

No Exceptions

Glancing over the menu at a local bowling alley, I decided to order the BLT. As I began to order, the clerk said, "Wait. That's not programmed on my cash register." He continued, "If it's not programmed into the cash register then we can't sell it to you." I explained that it was listed on the menu but he insisted that if it wasn't on the cash register then they couldn't sell it. What could this person have done to accommodate me? So much.

First of all, he should have apologized for the confusion. Secondly, he should have checked with a supervisor who could have assisted him. And workable as either a first or final solution, he could have taken my order by hand and asked me to have a seat while he checked to see how and if the order could be filled.

The conclusion of the story was that I didn't buy the BLT—or anything else. They simply lost my business because a salesperson didn't want to take an extra step. Actually, it wasn't even an *extra* step. There was no effort made to provide even the bare basics of customer service. The clerk clearly didn't see the parallel between my sale and his paycheck, and apparently didn't care that he lost the sale. Why should he? He was simply an employee!

> *"In business you get what you want by giving other people what they want."*
> ~ Alice MacDougall ~

Owning the business vs. working at the business—you would think the lines dividing those two would be firmly drawn. In many instances they are; but any frontline employee should be empowered with enough training and authority to solve a customer service issue as simple as this one. Whether it was completely employee error or partially that of management, it lends credence to those managers who advise their staff to "work like you own the company."

What exceptions have you been asked to make in your company? Has your staff been trained to handle these exceptions?

What Does the Policy Have To Do With Me?

I was in line at a fast food restaurant. I placed my order and drove to the second window, where I paid for the order and got my change. As the employee handed me the change, she asked if I would please pull around to the side while my order was being prepared. As I began to take off, I glanced in the rear view mirror and noticed that no one was behind me; so I asked the clerk why they were having me pull around. She explained that their restaurant was rated on how fast they get people through the line and they wanted me to pull around to help keep their numbers down.

Expedience is one thing. Nonsense is another. And while I'm certain that their company didn't see the request as nonsense, policies should not be implemented that inconvenience the customer. You know what happens when you pull around, when you're asked to move to that no man's land of the dreaded *first parking space*. They forget you...or they bring you the wrong order...or they don't include everything in your order and you either go home aggravated without them, or turn off the car and walk into the restaurant to have them correct the error. Worse yet, you don't realize they're missing until you get home, at which point you're *beyond* aggravated—and all of that pretty much defeats the purpose of a fast food drive-thru.

So, I said to the clerk, "I see your manager standing there. Can I speak with her, please?" She brought the manager to me and I briefly explained the situation. The manager smiled and pointed to a handwritten piece of paper above the register and said "See, it is our policy to have you move forward." Oh, okay, that explains it. Not.

First of all, the company knows something is wrong if you place an order for a meal that takes three minutes to cook and you are only in the drive-thru for 30 seconds. Secondly, is any of this really in the customer's interest? Now, if someone *had been* behind me, and they had a short order and could get in and out, that would be totally different.

I called the company's 800 number and explained the situation. They listened ...and they followed up by sending me a coupon for a free meal. I did not use the coupon because I did not *call* for the coupon. I just wanted to make them aware of the situation.

Talking Yourself Out of Money—But Into a Customer

Our garage door started acting up one day. As much as we tried, we could not get it to come down all of the way. I opened the phone book and scanned the pages for the local garage door company. I spoke with a female represesntative and asked to set up a service call. She briefly inquired about the problem, asking questions to help her pinpoint the problem. She said, "I would be more than happy to send out one of my technicians, but it would be a $65 service call. If you can take a moment to work with me, I might be able to assist you over the phone."

After just one minute, and at no cost, we had the problem resolved. She gave up a service call and the opportunity for her company to make $65. But what she *also* did was create a customer for life. We have used that company on multiple occasions and referred them to many of our friends. You see, they weren't just trying to make a buck; they were trying to assist a (potential) customer.

Putting On the Brakes

You've heard me say it before, I hate taking my car in to get it repaired for anything. It is a pain in the butt to take the car in, make arrangements for someone to pick you up, then take you back, and it just messes up your whole day. But, when my brakes were going out I knew I had no choice—that I was going to have to bite the bullet and make an appointment.

I called three local, reputable brake shops and asked about prices. Two quoted me the standard prices, but one said "Our price is _____, but we will also offer the following additional services at no extra charge:"

➤ Drive you to a destination of your choice (within 10 miles) and pick you up when you request
➤ Wash your car
➤ Vacuum out your car
➤ Provide a nice lounge (in case you wanted to wait) full of free refreshments, a big screen T.V., and wireless internet

I made my choice.

Gentle Reminders...Sturdy Incentives

Speaking of car maintenance, I am so pleased that my oil change company places that sticker inside my windshield or else I would probably never remember to get the oil changed at all. The company that I deal with offers a discount if you visit them within 3,200 miles of your last oil change. I asked them why they did that and they had three reasons:

➤ They are very interested in assisting in maintaining your car and frequent oil changes are important.
➤ The incentive encourages people to come in more frequently than they may have, which ultimately affects the bottom line.

➤ Each time a customer returns, they have the opportunity to WOW them. A WOW will often get them a referral.

Really, this is a small form of upselling. For me, knowing that I can save on the oil change with more frequent visits, I pay a little closer attention to the mileage on that sticker.

Maybe your company could do something similar to this. Your dry cleaner can provide a discount if you pick up your clothes within 72 hours. It helps them with inventory, and the sooner you have your items the sooner you wear them and the sooner you bring them back. This small method of upselling has a large impact on the bottom line.

The Road Less Traveled

We all go through our share of road construction. Don't you feel sorry for the sign holders? Standing there, looking like they are bored to death? What might you do differently if you were in that position? How about this?

➤ Smile
➤ Wave at drivers
➤ Make eye contact

Remember, the drivers do not want to be caught up in construction either so there is a huge opportunity for you to make their day. Yes, you will always have those drivers who are less than thrilled by your attempt, but forget about them. (They should have left the house earlier.) Make someone's day. Be different. Stand out. Send them to work with a smile instead of grumbling about the delays.

In your business, how can you make someone's day?

·We were in a restaurant and stopped a bus boy to ask, "Do you have any sugar?" He said, "Yes" and walked away, never to be seen again. What on earth was he thinking? That it was a rhetorical question?

Wrong

Our waiter was taking our order when he was approached by another waiter who said, "The customer at table five asked me to give you this." Our waiter turned to him and said, "Don't interrupt me when I am with other customers." Bad move on both their parts—and it's a perfect fit for the old cliché that two wrongs don't make a right. The second waiter should have never interrupted our waiter while taking an order. But equally in the wrong, our waiter shouldn't have berated another employee in front of us. Have you ever observed this or been a part of a similar situation? Remember, keep your internal issues internal.

It's Your Serve

I was at a hardware store and I was on a mission—shopping for a specific light fixture. I had seen one that I particularly liked at another of their store locations, but at that time I had not made my final decision. But after careful thinking, I finally decided on this particular fixture. When I asked the clerk if they had the fixture in stock, he said, "Do you have the product number?" and I said, "No." To which he replied, "You should have written it down." What?

I spent a few more minutes patiently describing the light—he said they were out. I asked if any of their other locations had the light—he said "I don't know." Okay then. I was getting a little weary of the verbal ping pong so I eventually gave up and left the store. My question is what could this clerk have done to assure the sale? He could have offered to contact another store, asked the store to ship it to their location, or ask if I was willing to go there to pick it up. Instead, he lost the sale. Did it matter to him? Probably not. His attitude indicated that it was just a job, and he failed to see how a sale equated to salary. Do you think his lack of any offering assistance would have changed if he had owned this hardware store? Probably.

❧

We were at an airport with a layover and decided to grab a bite to eat. There were eight of us, so we chose a restaurant that could seat all of us together. The hostess seated us and the waitress came over to take our order. She didn't allow us any time to look over the menu and stood and waited (impatiently) while we opened the menu to decide. She brought our drinks right before our meal and never came back. No refills. No checking to see how we were doing.

We finally were able to flag her down to get our bill. As she handed us the bill, she said "Remember, my tip is not included on this receipt so be sure to leave it on the table." Surely she didn't actually say that? She wants us to tip her for what? We left a tip but I doubt she was happy with it.

> *"Well, dinner would have been splendid...if the wine had been as cold as the soup, the beef as rare as the service, the brandy as old as the fish..."*
> ~ Sir Winston Churchill ~

We took my dad to a quality steak house to celebrate his recovery from an illness. He had recently been very sick and it was nice to just get him out of the house for an enjoyable dinner. There were eight of us in the party, and the waitress went around the table taking our drink order. She got to my dad, who was having trouble speaking. She asked him what he would like to drink, he told her, and she said, "WHAT?" So he repeated it. She said, "draft or bottle?" He told her, and she said, "WHAT?" It was so embarrassing, both for us and him. She had no idea how she was acting or how she made him feel. Then, when he was ordering his food, she kept interrupting him and not listening. We were very turned off by her service and therefore never returned. (We later learned that Dad had throat cancer. The waitress should not have assumed he was just whispering. Remember, you never know what is going on in a customer's life at that moment.)

"A sale is not something you pursue, it is something that happens to you while you are immersed in serving your customer."
~ Anonymous ~

Notes

Chapter Eight

Attention! Parade Rest...At Ease

Have Fun in Your Personal Life...
or How to *"Take a Sad Song and Make it Better"*

You need to have a balance of fun in your life. On the way home from a concert, we stopped at a gas station. Pulling next to the pump and getting out of the car, I couldn't help but "hear" (read that *be assaulted by*) the loud bass coming from the car next to us. The noise was so loud that our car was vibrating. So, I got back into the car and decided to take matters into my own hands. I dug through my CDs and found my favorite. I slid the CD into the player, turning the dials to max out both the bass and the volume. A timpani roll rumbled, and a loud but mellow voice intoned, "Ladies and Gentlemen, Mr. Barry Manilow!" Barry began singing, I began smiling, and the person next to me, with that crazy music, looked at me as if I had three eyes. I just laughed and broke out into song...thinking now that I should have added a dance routine to my performance.

Defusing a situation with humor can help take the stress off.

Leave Your Personal Life at Home, Please...

"I told you to put away those dishes and get your homework done!" Then she hangs up, just as your long wait in line has finally reached the counter. And something tells you that it's going to be impossible for the clerk to go from that conversation, leave it completely behind, and give you her full attention. Her thoughts are still caught up in what's happening, or *isn't* happening, at home. I understand that there are definitely times when we need to think about our personal life but maybe, *just maybe*, we could use work to forget about our personal problems or at least move away from them for a while. Really—what can we do about it while we are at work anyway? Nothing but worry.

From a personal point of view we might say, "But our personal life *is* part of our life;" but from the customer's point of view, do they really need to hear about it? Put yourself in the customers' shoes. Should they really have to hear about the relationship problem you are having? About family problems? Work problems?

Have you ever asked a customer service provider how they were doing and then wished that you hadn't? Oh, we have all been down that road. It is important for customer service providers to remember that the answer is not an invitation to complain or unload. It is an opportunity to say, "I'm having a great day. How are you today?" Really, what good does it do to whine about your own personal life, especially to the customer?

Presentation is Everything

The receptionist greets you with a wrinkled shirt. The dinner you've been served looks like the food was slopped on your plate. There is clutter all over the store. The inside of the trash cans hasn't been cleaned in months. Take a look at your company's overall presentation. What can you upgrade? What can be gotten rid of? What can be improved upon? Just make certain that it's not a one-time deal. Put the items on a schedule, make certain they're taken care of, then done again...and again...and again.

Ending is Everything

People remember the beginning and the end. So, you were able to start a nice conversation—that's great—but how did you end it? What options were there? How about:
- It was a pleasure meeting you.
- If there is anything else I can do, please let me know.
- Have a nice day and thank you for coming in.

You have the opportunity to leave a long, lasting impression. Do everything you can to guarantee that it's a great one.

Greeting

I often arrive at a certain restaurant for lunch right before they open. I wait outside (usually with other customers) until the clock hits 11:00 a.m. The door is always locked until the stroke of 11:00. When someone finally comes to the door, they turn the key from the inside then make an immediate about-face and go back in. What a mistake. Our first impression is *not* a good one.

What could they be doing? Minimally, they could hold the door open for us and greet us. They could smile and ask how we are doing and thank us for coming. That would be a great start…and so much better than staring at the employee's back as he walks away from the customers.

How are you greeting your customers?

How Many Times is Too Many?

If you are at the counter and someone comes in, of course you are going to greet them. But let's say that you work at a hardware store and the person keeps coming back because they need more supplies and more tools. On their fourth visit, do you greet them again? You bet! You can change up the greeting, even adding "welcome back" (to show that you remember them), but do not ignore them and feel it's justified because you're thinking, "Well, I greeted them once already." So what?

People tell me that when they walk down the hall, seeing the same person over and over again, they have chosen not to acknowledge them repeated times. Acknowledgement can be as effortless as a nod, a smile or simple eye contact. But there is no reason—or excuse—to ignore the person.

Who Doesn't Love Their Own Name

There is one thing almost everyone loves to hear—their own name. I'm not talking about the telemarketer who calls and says, "Is this Dawn Mushill?" I am talking about the business where they say, "Welcome back, Dawn. How many will there be today?"

There are so many times when the use of the name is appropriate. As you are checking out at the library, the desk clerk says, "Thank you, Mr. Smith, have a wonderful evening." This says that person paid attention and was actually in the moment.

In order to call the person Dawn vs. Mrs. Mushill, you should have been given permission by the person. In other words, she should say, "Please call me Dawn". Until she does that, you should refer to her by her last name. Examples include car rental, banks, airports, etc.

There are also times when use of the name is inappropriate, mostly due to confidentiality. If you work at a medical facility, you know what I am talking about. Please be aware of the use of the name.

Get to know your customers by name, and call them by their name whenever appropriate.

> *"It helps a ton when you learn people's names*
> *and don't butcher them*
> *when trying to pronounce them."*
> ~ Jerry Yang ~

Congratulations! – It's Important!

When my sister had her baby, I was a very excited aunt. I was in the delivery room with her, and something I will always remember is a nurse coming up to me and saying, "Congratulations, you are going to be a good aunt." As I understand it, that nurse had been employed at the hospital for over twenty years. Can you imagine how many babies she has assisted in the delivery room? But yet, at that moment, in the hospital, she impacted me more than she would ever know.

☙

My mom worked at a bowling alley for over thirty years. When people bowled a good game they would always run to tell her...and one day I realized why. As the bowlers described their games to her, regardless of the score, she would get excited right along with them. One day I watched as she congratulated a young girl, so excited that she had bowled a 100 game. Not so much to be thrilled about? For the girl, that was her best game ever. My mom gave hugs, high fives, or whatever she thought was appropriate. The other bartenders would get tired of hearing, "Where is Sue?" when the customers came to the window looking to share their story with her. No other bartenders ever caught on to the whole congratulations thing.

One of the best examples I have of congratulations is the time that I cut out the picture of a friend's child when it appeared in the newspaper. I laminated it and sent it to them, enclosing a personal note. The next day I received a call from the child. She said, "Dawn, thank you for taking the time to cut out my picture and send it to me. No one has ever done that for me." This girl had done something outstanding and deserved to be recognized. It was bittersweet to think that no one had acknowledged her before.

☙

My friend used to run a lottery machine. For eight hours a day, she stooped over a machine, inserted lottery cards, printed out tickets, and paid people. She said that the job became very mundane, very quickly. So, she tried to change it up a bit. Each time someone brought in a winning ticket (whether it was $2 or $1,200), she smiled, looked them in the eye, and sincerely congratulated them. She felt better because *they* felt better. When I asked her how she stayed so positive, she said, "When I win the big one, I want people to be excited for me too."

I have had many opportunities in my life to get excited; but unfortunately, on occasion I have failed my customer. I coordinate ribbon cuttings for people opening new businesses and, large or small, these are important events. Once I found myself at a ribbon cutting just standing there, not very excited, not really connected to what was happening. I'm not certain if it was the type of business or if I was just having a bad moment. Until someone said to me, "Remember that the ribbon cutting is the opening of a business which they have put their heart and soul into." And from that day on, I now celebrate each ribbon cutting with all of the participants in attendance. I remain in the moment, and I am genuinely excited for everyone.

The big trend of the past several years has been public karaoke. Some sing well and others...well, let's just stop there. But good or bad, it takes a huge amount of guts to get up in front of people and sing. The karaoke DJ's responsibility is to introduce the singer and play the music. But, what else could he do to encourage them? When he calls the person to the stage, he should do it with enthusiasm. Once the person is in front of the microphone, he could lend some moral support—whisper to them, "If you need me to help at any time, just give me the signal and I'll be more than happy to help." When the song has finished, the DJ could work the crowd to clap and get excited. You see, it has nothing to do with the song; it has to do with the experience. A DJ once told me that all of his business is word of mouth and most of his business comes from people who see him in person. An excited DJ is a busy DJ.

It's All in the Cards

Have you ever received a handwritten card from a company with which you have done business? How did it make you feel? Special? In what instances would it be appropriate to send a handwritten card? Here are some ideas:

> <u>Sympathy card</u> – loss of a loved one. If you learn of the loss of a loved one, maybe through the obituaries or through a friend, take a moment to drop a card in the mail. Our local veterinarian also sends out sympathy cards for the loss of a pet.

> <u>Thank you card</u> – it could be anything as simple as thanking them for their business to thanking them for something special they did.

> <u>Birthday card</u> – if you know your client well enough, a birthday card would be very appropriate. Don't waste your time sending a generic card with a printed signature. Take the time to actually sign the card, even including a short personalized note.

> <u>Get well card</u> – Are you aware that your customer had a surgery? Have they been out of work a few days with the flu? Send them a card wishing them a full recovery.

> <u>Referral cards</u> – People who make referrals to you deserve a handwritten card. Heck, that is free marketing for your company! Either verbally or

written, you should ask people how they heard about you.

> <u>Thinking of you card</u> – Maybe you see the person within the community and clearly they have their mind focused on something else. Maybe you read where someone in their family was in an accident. The "thinking of you card" says just that – you know they are going through a hard time and you just wanted them to know that you were thinking about them. If you own an insurance company, you know when there has been an accident. Let them know that you are there for them.

After reading this, you may think that you haven't developed a relationship that you would feel comfortable sending any of the above cards because they are quite "personal". My only question is why haven't you taken the time to develop a personal relationship?

Acknowledgements

Most of us would admit that we like to be acknowledged. Whether that is through written cards, in public or in person, we like to be recognized for an accomplishment. Who should we acknowledge? Well, those who most deserve it. Why do we sometimes forget to do so? Because we get busy and in a hurry. Who is responsible for acknowledging? Everyone.

It is amazing to me that people will write to companies about the poor service they receive, but usually fail to even *think* of writing to commend the great service they receive. The next time you're the recipient of service that exceeds your expectations, take a moment to write a letter to the manager and a card to the employee. Someone might return the favor someday—but if not, you'll still feel great for having done so.

Sometimes the acknowledgements are not happy ones. We recently lost one of our cats, and we were heartbroken. As we left the vet's office, they said how sorry they were; and when we started to pay our bill for that evening they said, "No, not now, it is not the time." Two days later in the mail we received a sympathy card from them, and it really touched us. You know how important your pet is to your family. They do too.

Does an acknowledgement always have to cost? Absolutely not. A personal "great job" is a start. How about leaving a "great job" paper, with a short note, on the person's desk? What about a special candy bar or cup of coffee?

When I receive excellent service (and I mean *excellent*), I will write a note on the back of my business card and give it to the service provider, with a "thank you for serving me today – you did great." I ask them to pass the card along to their supervisor. Usually, the supervisor will give me a call and thank me for taking the time to acknowledge their employee. Employees have even received rewards for something as simple as my taking just a moment to acknowledge them.

Earlier in my career, I would walk over to a fast food restaurant and get a salad and a diet soda for lunch. Unfortunately for me, I went to the restaurant at the same time the local high school students did. When I arrived there were always tons of kids, and I would patiently stand in line while the students made their way to the counter. While I was waiting I noticed something strange. The counter person knew each kid by name. Not only did she know them all by name, but she knew what they usually ordered. I'll never forget that one time she said to the customer, "You know, tonight your mom works late—so did you want the usual extra side salad?"

Okay, I am in a fast food restaurant where the lady knows all of her customers? The high school kids love her. They brought her class pictures (for which she had a huge wallet full of them)—they brought her cards—and they just enjoyed the time with her.

So, because I was so impressed with her, I wrote to the company's corporate office. I explained all that she did, and most importantly (to the corporate mind) how one person was so affecting the positive end of their bottom line. A few weeks went by before I returned...and when I walked into the restaurant I didn't see her behind the counter. But a second later I turned and saw her standing next to me, getting ready to hug me. You see, the corporation recognized her efforts and sent her a "diamond" pin to be added to her nametag. The fact that it wasn't a real diamond had nothing to do with this story. From the look on her face, you would have thought she received the real thing. She said to me, "No one has ever taken the time to do what you did. Thank you." I smiled and said, "No, thank *you.*"

Interestingly enough, not long after that interaction, I noticed that this employee no longer worked at that company. Apparently, a competitor's corporate vice president was at her fast food restaurant and noticed her dedication and her ability to bring in customers. So, without hesitation, he offered her a $4/hour raise; and she went with the new company. You can now go to her original fast food restaurant basically any time at all without waiting. You see, the rest of the staff never "got it"—they never developed that kind of relationship with the kids. In fact they often resented her because of the high standards she set for them, and that attitude translated to lost business.

As important as it is to acknowledge those who do well, it is just as important to acknowledge those who do not. For example, let's say that you receive horrible service at a local business. If you do not tell them what is wrong, they won't know about it and they can't change it. Some people write letters, others complain to managers, and some do nothing at all. If you write a letter, be sure to keep it brief while giving as many specific points as possible. Also, if you wish to be contacted, leave a telephone number where they can reach you during the day.

Remember to acknowledge people as deserved.

What if I am the Last Person to Receive the Thank You Note

Have you ever had to write a ton of thank you notes? You know how hard it is to keep things interesting. You start off with great intentions writing the first note:

Dear Bob and Carol:

Thank you so much for the lovely vase. We already have it filled with fresh flowers from our garden. It was great to see you at the wedding. The day was everything we imagined, and we were so happy that you could be a part of it.

Sam and Kris

By the 40th note, it is not quite as exciting:

Dear Bill and Jean:

Thank you so much for the gift and joining us at the wedding. The event was great.

Sam and Kris

By the 103rd note, it is just awful:

Dear John and Jodi:

Thanks for the gift.

Sam and Kris

You are tired of writing. You are hungry. You just want this to be over with. Your hand is cramping and you doubt that you'll ever be able to straighten your fingers again. And regardless of how great and personal the notes were to begin with, once you mail them everyone receives just their own—and John and Jodi are probably not going to be very impressed.

This is no different than assisting someone at your company. At the start of business you are excited that they are there, welcoming them. By the end of your shift, you are tired and you want to go home; but the clients you deal with then deserve the same service as those in the first part of your shift.

※

I had always loved a particular baseball player...and I noticed one Saturday that he would be signing autographs. I loaded up my old ball glove and stood in line in the hot sun for three hours, jammed in with all the other fans who were remembering favorite plays and citing statistics. But, to my disappointment, when I finally arrived at the autograph table, the person assisting the player grabbed my glove and shoved it in front of my "idol." The ball player signed it and never even looked up. For three hours I had stood in line as a fan, and I walked away from the table no more than a number. It wasn't so much the autograph but the *experience* that I was waiting for, and it just didn't happen. From a ball player's point of view, I understand how unexciting a situation like this can be for them. But what they have to keep in mind is that I am forming an impression of them as soon we come into contact. And in a round about way, I am paying their salary.

Recognition

In a business world where the competition levels range from mild to fierce, the issue of customer recognition should be elevated to essential policy, rather than just a casual consideration—especially if your goal is to provide the entire customer experience. If you don't, your competition will. How and when you recognize customers for their accomplishments allows for many possibilities and varies greatly based on the nature of your company's services. Gift certificates and discounted service are both easy on effort, and often work beyond the "thank you" to create repeat business. Outside the corporate realm, you can easily acknowledge their personal accomplishments, those of their family or those of their business.

With employees, sometimes it is the little things to recognize that mean the most. I once noticed an employee pushing a wheelchair-bound customer out to their car. On his way back, he was smiling. I told him how impressed I was by his courtesy, and he simply said, "It makes my day to help customers. That's why I'm here." Wow. Now there's a five-star attitude. I wrote to the manager and explained the situation, commending both the company and the employee for doing something so right—when it's those little things that are often so easily overlooked. I received a letter in response thanking me, stating that all of their employees work very hard to go the extra mile. The next week I saw the employee's picture on the wall, and next to it was my letter. I am sure that recognition went a long way...for all of us.

What programs do you have in place to recognize your employees?

> *"Without great employees*
> *you can never have great customer service."*
> ~ Richard F. Gerson ~

It's All About the First Impression

You only have three (3) seconds to make a first impression. Don't believe me? The next time you encounter a stranger, start the countdown and decide how long it takes for you to form an impression of them. Okay, so we can agree on three seconds then? And within that nearly non-existent amount of time you too will be completely evaluated, the person on the receiving end will be scrutinizing everything from body language, mannerisms, physical/verbal...every little detail from your haircut to your shoes. It's only human nature to do so. We're visual creatures, and the visual perception leaves a strong imprint. How come so many people blow it? Well, because we have many *opportunities* to blow it—via telephone, in person, or even on the internet.

Have you ever made a judgment of someone immediately (within three seconds)? Think about how you arrived at that impression. Was it the tone of voice? Was it the clothes? Was it the typo on the home page of their website? What could they have done (or not done) to make a great first impression? A smile in their voice is priceless. A smile says, "Welcome, we are glad to serve you."

Think about the last time you were impressed by someone within the first three seconds of meeting them. What was it that impressed you? The smile? The eye contact? The confidence or attitude? What first impression do others draw of you, when meeting you for the first time?

Appearance makes for a complex and interesting subject, whether you denounce or support that "you can't judge a book by its cover." I have a friend who is extremely attractive and another who is more plain. When they walk into a room together, everyone focuses on the more attractive of the two. Not too difficult to imagine *that* reaction, but here is the problem. She is so pretty that people seldom think beyond her appearance to discover that she is very intelligent as well. The other girl, on the other hand, is very plain; and people seldom recognize her intelligence either. You would think that basic human nature would flip the assessment on that one, equating pretty to dumb and plain to brainy. But they missed on both accounts. So, let's see how we might assist with the first impression.

Here are some tips:

➢ I just cannot say it enough—when meeting someone, give them a solid handshake, pointing your thumb to the sky and forming a 90 degree "L". And when I say solid, I mean solid, not fishy and not hurtful. I know some very, very influential people who have the dullest, limpest handshake that you could ever imagine. What they don't understand is that people are making an impression of them with the handshake alone.

➢ The handshake does not stand alone. There should also be eye contact, a solid posture, and a step into the handshake. Also, the obvious, your hands should be clean and not sticky or visibly dirty.

➢ Let's go beyond the handshake. Some people do not like nametags. I, on the other hand, love them. I am a visual person and often have a better recall of names if I see them in writing. The nametag should represent your business. How about using it as a marketing tool? You can include the company logo and the employee's name and tenure. Not only will you leave a lasting impression of your own name, but your company's name as well. The nametag can also provide a visual and memorable sense of your company. For example: at a networking event I attended, a company that sold fish had used that shape for all their marketing material that evening, including their nametags. Very clever—it's hard to forget a fish-shaped name tag. There was another company that had all of their realtor nametags designed in the shape of a house with a "sold" sign on them. Once again, very creative and clever.

➢ Be careful with your tone of voice. I tend to talk very quickly and a little louder than most. This turns off many people. So, I make a conscious effort to "tone down" my voice, especially in a large room of people. When appropriate, your voice should sound compassionate, confident, and knowledgeable. Prior to hanging up the telephone, people on the other end should feel as if they want to call you back because you were so helpful.

※

Have you ever gone into a business and drawn an impression as soon as you walked in the door? We probably all have. Sometimes it is a particular smell. Sometimes it is the way people acknowledge you (or don't). Other times it is the cleanliness of the building, the facial expression of the employees, the noise, the quiet, etc.

On a recent visit to a restaurant, as soon as we pulled into the parking lot we noticed several pieces of trash, including broken bottles. We parked our car and entered the building, passing a bulletin board in the outer vestibule where people had placed cards, flyers, and brochures. It was overflowing, unstructured, unorganized, with cards two and three deep and out-of-date flyers. They had a slot where the pay phone used to be and it was covered with a trash bag. The entrance was dusty and the mat hadn't been changed in quite a while. The glass on the entrance door clearly hadn't been cleaned in a long time.

But we kept moving forward and entered the restaurant. There was a hostess station—but no hostess anywhere to be found. Our wait was a relatively short one compared to some, but even thirty seconds can feel long when you're the one who is waiting. When she approached us, we didn't realize that her disinterested "Two?" would be the full extent of her conversation with us; and while we sat at the table she'd given us, studying the menu and discussing our experience so far, we glanced around the restaurant. The main thing to draw our attention was a sign that read, "We pride ourselves on: Service, Cleanliness, Great Food, and Great Prices." Okay—well we were definitely looking forward to those *last* two promises because we sure hadn't seen the first.

At this point, it would have taken a miracle to turn this evening into a positive one. We had already started to develop the experience in our head, and it was leaving a heavy imprint. Seeing the lack of attention to detail made us wonder how they handled the food. Would we dare use the bathroom?

As we left, we once again toured the overflowing bulletin boards, the trash bag on the wall, the dusty mat, and the dirty glass. We hope, since then, the restaurant has "seen" these errors—has had the opportunity to *be their own customer* in a sense, and paid attention to such glaring details. They could use some major help on their "first impression" especially when it's also their last.

⚜

We were looking for a new cleaning company, and we decided to visit a number of competitive businesses to compare price, gain a first impression, etc. We walked into the office of the first company to acquire a quote. As I looked up, I could see that all the air vents were packed with dust, and my first impression settled in. There were a number of other cleaning issues that were definitely "off," including that the trash in the restroom was overflowing. It was obvious that what they did for a living they were *not* doing for their own office; and I couldn't trust them with the appearance of ours. Once again another company that could have benefited greatly by looking at their business through their customers' eyes.

What is your company's first impression? Have you checked your parking lot? Your bulletin board? Your lobby? Your front-line staff? Remember to exceed the customer's expectations within the first three seconds. It's usually a pop quiz, it's the fastest test you'll ever take, and it's nearly always a pass/fail grade.

What can you add to this list?
➢ Clear/clean signage with logo, address, phone number, and website listed
➢ All light bulbs in working order
➢ Clean entrance
➢ Parking lot free of garbage (if you tend to have a lot of trash in the parking lot, you should supply additional trash cans)
➢ List your hours on your door (or when you will return) along with your website address

Ask your closest friend to tell you about the first impression you make, giving you two things that they believe you could improve on. A good friend who wants to see you succeed will be honest enough to help you.

Notes

Chapter Nine

The Large and Small of It

"The devil is in the details..."
~ Hyman George Rickover ~

Takin' Care of Business

Little things add up. *Good* little things can touch your heart and be an unexpected pleasure. *Bad* little things can grow up to be a major aggravation; and if you get enough bad things gathered together they can bully and annoy you until you have a major case of mob reaction on your hands...the attack of the insignificant. Ultimately, your business will suffer the casualties. While many organizations emphasize focus on the big picture, it's those seemingly unimportant things that, overall, can have the greatest impact. Unimportant to whom? You have to remember that it's only a minor inconvenience if it's happening to someone else.

If the little things are left ignored, you're sending an engraved invitation for customer dissatisfaction; while dedicated attention to detail sends the message that your customers are important. You don't have to overdo it—you don't have to hover or suffocate with kindness. Just be real. Recognize and implement the truth that it's those small things that can make the biggest difference. Don't slide by with doing less, when you have the easy option to do more.

What small details can you focus on or enhance to make your company a standout?

"Little things make big things happen"
~ John Wooden ~

It's in the Name

My favorite job title of all time, and one I never expected to find, was "Director of First Impressions." Actually all of us could hold that title; but in this particular instance it was held by a receptionist. When I asked her about it, she said that she was very proud of the title, honored that the first impression she gave to the client was the one that they would remember forever. She said she worked hard at putting a smile in her voice, answering the phone within two rings and providing the client with more than they expected.

What creative titles can you come up with for the staff at your business?

Make Them Feel at Home

What do you do when you have company in your home? You make sure that the house is clean and all rooms are nicely decorated. In the bathroom you pay special attention to make sure there are clean towels, plenty of toilet tissue, fresh smelling soap, pretty decorations, vacuumed carpeting, etc.

You greet your company at the door, often with a handshake or hug depending on who they are and what's appropriate. You walk with them through the house and invite them to sit down, offering something to drink (with the smell of fresh coffee being brewed) and maybe a snack. You draw them into relaxed conversation, about current events or things you may have in common. Together you enjoy the evening and at the end, you walk them to the door. The next day, you follow up with a short note, thanking them for a wonderful evening. It's basic manners 101.

Now, let's put this into a business perspective. What could you do to enhance your experience with your clients? The same as above—minus the hug. Think of your customers as friends coming into your own home...your *business* home... and on a professional level extend the same courtesies, respect, and interest.

When You Err

It happens. As hard as you work for it *not* to happen, it happens. I've done it, you've done it, we all have done it.

> ➤ You are hoping to make that great first impression and you call the president of the company by the wrong name.
> ➤ You are giving a presentation to a group of five hundred and you use the wrong company name (their competitor).
> ➤ You need to vent about a customer so you invite your best friend to lunch. As you are in the middle of your story, you notice the customer sitting behind your best friend, knowing the customer heard everything.

> ➤ Your mouse clicked on "send to all" instead
> of "send" and your frustrations were sent
> throughout the company.

What can you do? Well, you can start with "I am sorry" and own up to your mistake. That three-word phrase goes a long way. You can also follow up with flowers, candy, notes – whatever you think would be appropriate. The error will also help you think about things you say (once they are out, they cannot be retracted).

We all make mistakes...but how you rectify them can make or break a situation.

> *"If you're not making mistakes,*
> *then you're not doing anything.*
> *I'm positive that a doer makes mistakes."*
> ~ John Wooden ~

Everyone is a Potential Customer

One Sunday afternoon I was in the middle of baking when I ran out of milk, so I made a quick jaunt to the grocery store. It was just going to be a fast in-and-out trip, but another customer in the store walked up to me and said, "Aren't you the person who spoke at the women's meeting last week?" I smiled and said, "Yes, I am." She responded, "I thought you were great." We chatted a bit about the subject, I introduced myself to her children, and then off we went in our separate directions.

A couple of days later I received a call from the president of a local company. He said that his wife had heard me speak at the women's meeting a couple of weeks ago and he would like to hire me. He further mentioned that his wife ran into me at the grocery store, and she had been so impressed by the time I spent with her that he knew I was the right person to provide customer service training. They remain my largest client.

Closing Time

Exactly what time *is* closing time? If a restaurant says that it closes at 10:00, does that mean it doesn't serve food after 10:00 or it doesn't seat people after 10:00?

I was at a local card store picking up some last minute birthday cards. I arrived at 8:30 p.m., a half hour before closing time. At 8:40 they announced the store would be closing in twenty minutes. At 8:45 they announced the store would be closing in fifteen minutes. At 8:50 they announced the store would be closing in ten minutes. At 8:55 they announced that the store would be closing in five minutes. I made my way up to the checkout at 8:50. I placed my items on the counter and the checker began ringing up my order. At 8:58 the checker said to the other clerk, "Get the door!" and the clerk ran over to the door and locked it. Apparently she had seen a customer walking toward the store and wanted to make certain that she didn't get in. The clerk didn't say a word to the customer, simply locked the door in her face.

I was in line at a grocery store. I unloaded everything from my cart onto the conveyor, and as I approached the checker she said, "I'm leaving for the day. You'll have to go to another line." Could she not have told me that before I unloaded my groceries? How about taking a few minutes to go ahead and check me out?

It's simple. People remember how you treat them—and a bad experience keeps many customers from returning.

Give Me Some Direction

Have you ever walked into a restaurant and were uncertain if you were to seat yourself or wait to be seated by a hostess or server? What could the company have done to lessen the confusion? How about better signage? I worked with a company whose employees became so frustrated because people constantly asked where the restroom was. At their team meeting I said, "What can we do to eliminate this question?" No one had an answer. So, I put it to them in a different way. I said, "I train at another company where people constantly ask where the Customer Service Department is. The employees there also became frustrated with the same question over and over. What do you think they can do?" Immediately seven hands went up and they all had the same answer – put up a sign. Okay. It's ironic that they couldn't see it for their own business because they were so close to the situation, but they were quick to identify a solution for someone else.

At a convenience store a clerk became very frustrated because people kept asking her the price of a special candy that was displayed near the register. You could see the aggravation on her face every time someone asked the price. What was obvious to me (put the price on the front of the display) was *not* obvious to her. Remember, if you receive the same question over and over, instead of being frustrated with the customer, think about what you can do to correct the situation.

What questions are you receiving consistently? What can you do to assist the customer?

What's Best for the Customer

A business acquaintance of mine opened a sewing shop in January, and by April her business was still very slow. She came to me for assistance, so I stopped by the shop. Before I even walked in the door to talk with her, I noticed her posted hours were Tuesdays through Friday from 10:00 a.m. until 2:00 p.m.—and that's exactly how part of our conversation began: with me asking about the hours and whether she thought they were convenient for the customer. "I can't help it," she said. "I can't work any more hours than that." She said she needed to drop her kids off at school and run some errands before coming to work, and then be able to pick her kids up again at 3:00 p.m. "If they want sewing equipment then they will have to come between 10:00 and 2:00." I imagine many people *did* want and need the equipment, and the shop was a great addition to the area. But it became a moot point. Her very limited four hours, from mid-morning to mid-afternoon, apparently weren't compatible with the majority of customers' schedules. She is no longer in business.

⚜

I remember when banks were not open on Saturdays, but to accommodate their customers they stayed open (at least their drive-thru) until 7:00 p.m. on weekdays. Once they opened on Saturdays, many began closing at 6:00 p.m. during the week (or even earlier). So, you leave your house at 7:30 a.m. to be at work by 8:30 a.m. in another city. You finish working at 5:00 p.m. and have to pick the kids up at daycare by 5:45, which gives you a very small window of time to drive by your bank.

I know, many transactions can be made online; but let's say that you have a check in your hand and need to make a deposit. At this point your only hope is to go to the bank on Saturday. But you work until noon. Too bad. Those are the bank's hours. I know, right now all of the bank employees reading this are saying, "How would you like to work until 7:00 p.m. each night?" Let's try a different scenario.

How many times have you had to take off work to go to the doctor? Why do doctors not understand that they are like everyone else and try to better accommodate the customer's schedule. How about the following doctor's office hours:

Monday – 8:00 a.m. – 5:00 p.m.
Tuesday – 10:00 a.m. – 7:00 p.m.
Wednesday – 8:00 a.m. – 5:00 p.m.
Thursday - CLOSED
Friday – 7:00 a.m. – 4:00 p.m.
Saturday – 9:00 a.m. – 2:00 p.m.
Sunday – CLOSED

This allows for people to go in before work (Friday) and after work (Tuesday). It still allows for those who don't work to schedule appointments during the day and really accommodates anyone on Saturday. Again, if you work for a doctor's office you are probably not going to like the hours above; but it is really about making yourself accessible to the customer.

A local drug store was struggling as it faced competition from two larger pharmacies, both of which were open 24 hours a day. Because of those business pressures they were forced to cut both staff and pharmacy hours. While the pharmacy had once remained open from 9:00 a.m. until 7:00 p.m., it now closed at 4:00 p.m. and was only open until noon on

Saturday. When did they expect people who worked to be able to pick up their prescriptions?

Take a look at your competitors. What are their hours? What are they doing for the customer, above and beyond? Take notes and implement when possible. Try to get out of the nine-to-five mentality and decide what is the best time to serve your customers. By doing so, you'll see an increase in business and revenue.

Treat Us as People

I was sixth in line at the grocery store, with four additional people behind me. The person currently being waited on asked the checker if she noticed the long line. The checker responded with, "they are just going to have to wait. I can only do one thing at a time." As you can imagine, the experience for the rest of those in line was not a positive one.

Interestingly enough, the next day I happened to be behind this same lady (the checker from the grocery store) in line at the dry cleaners. She was third in line and turned around to me and said, "You would think they would see how long this line is. I have to get to work." Too funny. It's the little things.

❧

At a former doctor's office, I always knew that the wait was going to be a long one. Usually from start to finish I was there at least two hours. I understand that the doctor is busy, possibly even called out for a delivery, but I always wonder if *he* would like to sit and wait that long.

One day I had been waiting for about twenty minutes when the receptionist opened the window and yelled out, "Dr.

Grant is delivering a baby and all appointments will be an hour and a half late. If you do not want to wait, please step up to the window and we can reschedule." Although I didn't think the approach was perfect, I did appreciate the opportunity of choice to reschedule or to wait (and to know just how long the wait would be).

Think about your customers' needs.

Suggestions for the Healthcare Industry

> I know this is often out of your control, but during a hospitalization it would be of huge assistance from the family's point of view to know a time frame the doctor may arrive. (Hospital staff have indicated to me that they usually have no idea when the doctor will be present, so it would be up to the doctor or his office to keep them informed.) We have jobs and lives and any number of demands on our time too; and it is not always in *our* control to stay there 24/7 waiting on a doctor's visit.

> Staff and doctors should refrain from mentioning a release date prematurely. On day seven, someone on staff suggested the possibility of going home soon; but instead, the family member was in the hospital an additional three weeks. The patient had a full two weeks of disappointment and false hope, thinking each day would be the one to get out of the hospital.

> Listen to the patient—double-check the chart. A patient told the nurse he could not have liquid, but she insisted he could and gave it to him

anyway. When he got to testing they said he should not have had anything to drink, nothing liquid at all—and further delays ensued. He was also given five different medications, even after explaining to the nurse that earlier that morning the doctor had taken him off two of them. She told him to go ahead and take all five. Later, another nurse came in and told him he should not have taken the two additional pills.

➤ Watch for signs. For ten days, Dad didn't eat anything on his plate. The dietary staff would bring in his plate and later return to pick it up untouched. No one said a word. One day a more attentive dietary aid said, "Mr. Johnson, it doesn't look like you are eating very much." That was on day ten of no eating. He noted that it was too hard to swallow. The dietary aide spoke with the nurse who in turn spoke with the doctor. They did a few tests and found out he had throat cancer. Finally someone had taken the time to observe and follow up.

➤ Many on staff throughout the hospital do a poor job of acknowledging people in the hallway.

➤ When having tests done, it would be great to know how long it will take to determine the results. This can be mentioned to the family if they are in the room when the patient leaves for testing.

➤ Offer wireless Internet in the room and provide the password needed.

- ➢ Offer plenty of television channels. (You try lying in a hospital bed for 27 days with only four stations to watch.)
- ➢ Provide a resource person who can answer questions regarding home healthcare, billing issues, care questions, etc. During one of my dad's hospitalizations, it would have been nice to have someone contact us who was consistent with these resources. If there was someone assigned to his case in this capacity, we were never informed of it and didn't know to ask.
- ➢ Staff members now carry cell phones which act as an interoffice method of communication. A good tool, especially in emergency situations, but it should not be answered when talking with a patient or his family. Again as a firsthand experience, some people answered their cell right in the middle of a conversation we were having with them.
- ➢ If they announce someone over the intercom, they should end the page with a release button and not just hang up the phone.
- ➢ Someone should clean the room by sweeping, mopping, and wiping down the bed. Because it is not always obvious, a note should be left noting that housekeeping was there (just like at a hotel).
- ➢ Make sure all people who are authorized are trained on equipment. Some nurses struggle with IV drip machines and are clearly not properly trained.

➢ Be consistent with rules. Are restrooms in the patient's room for patients only? Some staff say yes and others say no. Are visiting hours strictly from 10 a.m. until 7 p.m.? Are extended hours allowed for immediate family?

➢ As a manager, challenge each staff member after an eight-hour day to tell you one unique thing about the patient or the family. That will help you determine if they are really trying to develop relationships and provide personal and attentive care.

➢ Patients should be acknowledged each and every hour. This can be done with someone from dietary, housekeeping, nursing, admissions or any other department. This will assist in decreasing your call lights.

➢ When returning the patient to the room after x-rays or other tests, ask the family to step out and say to them, "We are going to get him settled if you would want to take a little break."

➢ Try not to expose the catheter bag. Just because exposing it makes it easier for you to monitor doesn't mean that either the patient or the family want to stare at it all day. Please give them all some dignity.

As a healthcare professional, what changes could you make? If you are *not* in healthcare, what changes above can you incorporate into your own business?

Missed Opportunities

Every day I see it—the missed opportunity—the chance to make the customer's visit an "experience." There are so many perfect openings for a company to give its customers service that would set them apart, but too often little time is given to the moment. The opportunity is lost, and the chance for memorable and impressive customer service goes right along with it.

> "Opportunity is missed by most because it is dressed in overalls and looks like work."
> ~ Thomas Alva Edison ~

But it really doesn't have to be such hard work. Think of it as "downtime" turned into "relationship building" time. By simplest definition, the most frequently occurring "missed opportunity" is a moment lost during which you could begin developing a relationship. Albeit, at times a short-term one, but you can certainly lay the groundwork for long-term ones as well. Here are some examples:

> ➢ You are sitting in a doctor's waiting room and there is nothing to do. What if there were appropriate wall posters, general information posted in the area or inspiring poems on the wall? How about when you enter the examination room? Why are there usually only white walls to stare at? The anatomy posters I can understand, and at least they add some color—but think about what else could be displayed on those walls. Remember, time goes by very slowly for the patient when he is just sitting and waiting.
> ➢ How about the checker who scans your items but doesn't say a word? What could she be asking?

What might she have in common with you that could spark a good conversation?

> The gas station attendant who takes your money, returns your change, and makes zero conversation.

> The hostess is taking you to your seat in a restaurant and simply walks five feet ahead of you. How about mentioning the specials...or asking you if this is your first time at this restaurant...thanking you for coming?

> When people ask a question such as "Where is the restroom?" it would be best to take them there (vs. simply telling them where it is). While you are walking with them (not in front of them or behind them), strike up a conversation. *Have you been finding everything okay? It sure is a beautiful day. Did you see our sales advertisement? Our (sports) team is sure doing great this year. Do you follow their games?* If you do not have a clue as to what conversation to make, take a real look at your customers. Maybe they can give you a hint by what they are wearing. Do they have a sports shirt on? Do they have jewelry that you can compliment them on? Does their sweater look handmade? Is there a picture of their grandchildren on their keychain?

> Have you ever won a jackpot at a casino and been paid by an attendant? What a missed opportunity when he simply pays you and asks you to sign the slip. The attendant should be excited and congratulate the winner. Anyone

else involved in the transaction (i.e. the security guard, a supervisor, etc.) should also be excited. It doesn't matter if these employees have paid off seventy-five people that day; this person is important *at that moment* and deserves to have the people surrounding them excited for them too.

➤ When I turned in a scratch-off lottery ticket for which I won $20, the clerk said to me, "I never win anything. I have bought tickets for years and never won anything. You walk in the door, pick a ticket and win $20. That is so unfair." That is not at all how the conversation should have gone. It should have been more to the tune of "Congratulations on your win! This must be your lucky day."

➤ You go to a hardware store in need of a specific item, only to find the clerk and be told that the product is out of stock. The clerk says, "I will be right back" and goes to the hardware store next door to make the purchase. He returns, rings it up, and everyone is happy. WOW!

➤ When customers ask you where a particular item is, take them there rather than just pointing in the direction of the product. Make conversation with them while you are walking.

➤ If children are present, be sure to address them directly and ask them something age appropriate. Make them feel noticed—important. Maybe you can ask them about a particular movie character (often children wear a character they like right on their shirts).

You should utilize each and every opportunity to interact with your customers.

Don't Forget About the Travelers

I have been traveling a lot over the last few years, and have discovered that there are companies who exclusively cater to travelers. For example, when we took a cruise our expectations were at an all-time high—fun, fun, fun. The one thing we failed to consider was that for those who *work* on a cruise ship, it is just their job.

We had always seen on T.V. how the passengers were welcomed with leis, and we received ours as we boarded the ship. We knew all about the sumptuous buffets, with incredible food presented like artwork, formed into exotic animals and other amazing designs. We saw that, and definitely enjoyed sampling our share of it. We had learned about the little luxury touches—bath linens folded into animal shapes—the origami of the towel world—and we saw those too. We had been fed image after image of staff who were all happy, always smiling, and ready to assist. Well—three out of four isn't bad. But remember, for them it is just a job. Just like for us, sometimes *our* job is just a job too.

Travelers like to take an enormous amount of pictures. Have a backdrop available for photo taking that includes your logo. What better way for them to remember their fun trip and have the picture to show exactly where it was taken. Have a sign-in book for visitors. Ask for their mailing and email addresses and send them a card after they leave, thanking them for stopping by. Send them an e-mail on a monthly or seasonal basis, showing what your company is featuring and what specials and discounts are available at that time. Stay in their mind...and you'll *be* in their mind when it is time to make the final plans for this year's vacation.

Have postcards available and provide one free of charge to every family. You can have additional postcards available for a small fee, but the first one should be gratis. Again, if they take it home for their scrapbook instead of mailing it to a friend, it could help to remind them how fun the vacation was.

Travelers love local maps. Provide a list of local restaurants, parks, gas stations and other pertinent information. Businesses can pay to have their information listed or you can include it as a complimentary service.

While traveling, as most people do, we stayed at a hotel. This hotel was like no other. As soon as we walked in, they had a fully-stocked mini bar with bottled water, soda, juice, and snacks. The sign said, "We know you have been traveling for a while and may just need a pick me up. Please enjoy." Wow. We haven't even checked in. As we approached the desk, the clerk had a great smile, acknowledged us with a greeting and said, "Welcome to XYZ Hotel." She extended her hand and said, "I am pleased that you chose our facility and my goal today is to exceed all of your expectations." What? We are at a hotel. We processed through the registration very quickly.

As we finished, we noticed a person approaching our luggage. He loaded it quietly and waited for us at the elevator, holding the door. The gentleman asked where we were from and suggested some local attractions that he thought we might enjoy. He held the elevator door open as we exited, made small talk all the way to our room, held open the door, put away the luggage, and quietly exited.

There was a plate of freshly baked cookies on a plate. The note said "Dear Sue, Terri, Dawn and Bailey. Thank you for choosing the XYZ hotel. We hope the cookies will tide you over until dinner." Oh...my...goodness. Everything was perfect. Even the shower head was amazing. There were plenty of towels, a coffee pot, coffee, an iron, a hair dryer, and even a microwave with microwave popcorn.

The price we paid (as if it really matters) was an average price for the hotels in the area. The service, though, was unbelievable; and I would challenge any hotel to consistently meet or exceed this level of service. Since that trip, we have always gone out of our way to stay at these hotels; and each and every time the staff exceeds our expectations. They have learned the secret of gaining and retaining business through exceptional service. Have you?

Notes

Notes

Chapter Ten

The View from the Top

"Good management is the art
of making problems so interesting
and their solutions so constructive
that everyone wants to get to work
and deal with them."

~ Paul Hawken ~

Why Do People Want to Work for Your Company?

Is your company a good one to work for? How do you know? Do you have people waiting in line to be hired? Do you have an impressive number of applications on file? Do some of the best employees apply? Do they ask that you keep their information on record and advise them of any future openings? What does your company offer to its employees that other companies do not? Think about being the best company in the world. What would it take? How close are you to getting there?

Keeping Busy

There is always something to do. Period. If you go into a business and see someone standing around, you can blame management (or the lack thereof). If you *are* the manager, make a list of five things your employees can do if they have five minutes, ten minutes or even twenty minutes on their hands. A lot can be accomplished in only a short period of time, and the list could nudge them in the right direction.

As a manager, are you keeping busy? What do you think when you walk into a business and people are just standing around? You do not want people to have that same perception of your business. Keep them busy.

Training Your Staff

We are all in the service business. You hire people who want or need a job. In addition to those basics, hopefully they also want to provide service. My belief is that you should hire people with passion, then teach them the skill they need to learn. How do you teach them? It begins on day one. Here are some tips:

> ➢ Help your staff to know the big picture – from start to finish.
> ➢ Let them see your passion. Let them see how hard you work every single day. You don't have to *tell* them, they'll see it for themselves.
> ➢ Provide a checklist for your new staff. They can check it off, initial it, and return it to you once completed. Be sure to review the checklist with them, answering any questions they may have and offering suggestions.
> ➢ Make sure the person providing the training is one of your best performers. If a mediocre employee trains the new hire, guess what is going to happen to the new hire?
> ➢ Evaluate the new trainee frequently, providing feedback and allowing them to ask questions. The questions shouldn't end after the initial

training. The more a person *knows* about a job, the more they'll know to ask. Questions are a good sign.

Also, be aware that you need to hire people who *own* their job versus rent their job. The difference? The job renters are only there for the paycheck. Owners really care.

Interview Questions

Hiring the right people is the absolute key to a successful business. The wrong employee can make or break you and make everyone miserable while getting to that point. If we want to be great then we need to ask great questions to get great people. Asking someone about their strengths and weaknesses is okay, but there are other questions that may take the conversation to an entirely different level:

➤ If you had a challenging customer, give me three things you might do to assist in the situation.
➤ How do you feel about emptying the trash?
➤ Share with me the last time you and another employee had a disagreement. Please role play the part your co-worker took and the role you played as well.
➤ If you are not feeling your best, how can you bring out the best in yourself before you see your first customer or co-worker?
➤ Who is the biggest influence in your life? What are his/her strengths and weaknesses?
➤ What is your biggest pet peeve concerning service employees?

> ➢ What is your biggest pet peeve with customers *you* are serving?

Let the interview questions work for you.

Put People in the Right Company Position

Sometimes I ask myself, "what were they thinking?" There is a store in town with a marquee signboard with letters that are placed by hand. One week the marquee said, "Hole chickens $.99/lb." Another week it read, "Pea Nut Butter $2.49". Still a third advertised, "All serial 20% off." I am not kidding. I know that Joe likes to do the marquee, but is he really the right person for that job if he can't spell? And even with his unique approach to spelling, if you still want Joe to continue to do the marquee, just write the information on a piece of paper for him.

Have you ever had an employee who really wasn't working out in one area so you moved them to another sector of the company? One of my clients had an employee who had worked for their company for three years; and in those three years she had been through several departments. One manager after another would move her around, not for reasons of promotion or cross-training, but simply so they did not have to deal with her. If you looked at her personnel file, everything seemed fine because her evaluations would be done by a new manager who had only worked with her for a short time. As a last resort, (maybe because every other position had been exhausted?) they had her answer the phones. Hello? First impression? Of course, it just didn't work out. She was not a people person from the very beginning and there was no chance of changing her.

Before placing someone in a position, make certain that they are the right person *for* the position. If not, both you and the employee will pay for it later.

⚜

A friend of mine had a true love of books. She read everything. She knew about authors, the best seller's list, about art... You would think she would be perfect for the library. But there was just one problem—she was very outgoing and very loud. Still, she interviewed well and took the job, only to be let go a week later. As much as she tried, as much as she loved the job, she just couldn't tone down her voice because she was so enthused about the books.

Would you agree with me when I say that there are many people in service that have clearly chosen the wrong profession? We have all experienced those awful customer service providers. It seems to me that very little training has gone into helping them to be qualified to work in the service industry—and it just doesn't make much sense.

Help your employees find their dream job. If they are great employees, hope that you can help them find it in your company. If they are *not* great employees, hope that you can help them find it in someone else's company.

Hire Staff with Passion – Knowledge Can be Trained

One of the best assistants I ever hired didn't know much about computers, but she did know a lot about people. We received so many compliments on her personal service, the way she handled situations, and how she treated people. You can train a person on computers and company policies, but you can't train them to have passion about their job.

What effect does passion have on job performance? How would the lack of passion be displayed in a job? You see it all of the time. Some people are there simply because they have to be in order to receive a paycheck.

Set Hiring Expectations High

I dealt with a company that was seeking my help with employee turnover problems. They historically went through a temporary agency for all of their employees, and after only a week people would quit. So much so that their ninety-day retention rate was less than 20%. I asked them what credentials they sought from the potential employees of the temporary agency. They said, "basically, they need to be breathing." So, whose fault was it that most of the employees sent by the temp agency were not working out? Well, I say it was the company's fault. Did the temporary service meet the expectations of the company? Yes, they did (assuming that everyone they sent was breathing).

Once new expectations were developed by the company, the temporary agency said they could no longer assist them. (Clearly their expectations for their employees were very low.) And once the company became established with a new temporary agency, their ninety-day retention rate exceeds 80%.

If you hire the right people, the rest will follow. Let's put it this way – if you hire the wrong people, it's all over but the crying. Have you ever hired the wrong person? Almost from day one, you begin to see what an uncomfortable fit it is for everyone. Expect excellence—then hire the people who match your expectations.

Chapter Eleven

Show Me the Money?...
or Show Me the Job

Choosing the Right Job

It is not about the money. Let me say that again—it is *not* about the money. Yes, I know, there is a certain minimum we all need to make. But in addition to a first-class salary, we are really seeking other things...respect, trust, a positive work environment, a feeling of accomplishment...the list is long.

People use money as the bottom line. A past intern of mine, who had an Associate Degree in Marketing, was offered two job opportunities upon completion of her internship: a clerk position at a law firm and a clerk position at a marketing firm. In some ways it was a difficult decision process. But the law firm paid $1.00 more per hour. Guess which job she took? After five months she called me and said "I really made a mistake. I hate going to work every day, and this job has nothing to do with what I went to school for."

A simple philosophy I live by today is that you should wake up every morning excited about going to work. Is that a little overboard? Maybe. I guess it would be better said that you should wake up most mornings *wanting* to go to work. Many people I've spoken with, those not fitting into the wanting-to-go-to-work pattern, would often tell me, "but I make too much money to leave" or "I have been here so long, no one else would hire me." Unlike those people who took the risk and made the move, leaving their higher paying job to do something they absolutely loved. In that situation, I have yet to meet anyone who said, "it was the wrong move." Again, I am talking about those people who really hate what they do.

A student of mine was going on an interview at a local casino and she was so excited. I helped her practice her interview questions, worked with her on her resume and cover letter, and even helped her pick out an outfit. She called me again after the interview, thrilled that it seemed to have gone so well. Then they called her back for a second interview, after which she accepted the job. Over the weekend, we celebrated. She began the following Monday morning, and at noon that day she called me. I asked her how she liked the job. She said, "I had to quit". I asked her why and she said, "I don't believe in gambling." She had gotten so caught up in the money that she hadn't really thought about her true passion, her own beliefs. But to give you a positive update, she has since found her passion – childcare.

I love when high school and college students job shadow—which involves spending some time with an employer in an industry in which they are interested. It is great to see the faces of the students who realize they have found their passion. But there are also those students who found the job to be something completely different than they had originally imagined. I had one student who wanted to be a veterinarian.

So on job shadow day she was so excited. She loved animals and had grown up with cats, dogs, and several other animals. After the job shadow day I noticed that she had quieted down; and when I asked her what was wrong she said, "I think I chose the wrong career. I love animals, but I don't like it when they are sick or hurt." Even so, she found a way to stay with her dream and now owns and operates five pet grooming businesses.

❀

Don't tell my husband, but in the late 1990s, I was offered a lucrative position as a corporate trainer. The annual salary was probably more than I will ever make in a year's time. But at that same time, we were just moving into our new house (that we had spent years building and planning), and we were very excited about it. The job required leaving town on Sunday night and traveling around the country all week to train in various locations. I would return home again each Friday evening.

Besides the impressive salary, the job paid all of my expenses—but there were some downsides. In addition to the travel, it was a five-year commitment. Could I really be excited about being in a hotel five nights a week? Did I really want to leave my family and miss all of the family events? No, not at all. But while I declined the job offer I never gave up my dream of training. Some time later I started my own company and just kept going from there. There are always options—always different directions possible in reaching the goal.

You could truly pay me $100,000, $200,000 or $300,000 a year and I would not be able to take a job in daycare. Why not? Primarily because I lack the skill to relate well or confidently manage groups of children. So it wouldn't be fair to anyone involved—children and grownups alike. No matter the amount of money I might make, I would be setting up both myself and my employer for failure. A bad fit in career choice would have me dreading going to work every day, being miserable; and that couldn't help but spill over into my personal life.

The moral of the story? It is as important to know what you love as it is to know what you *do not* love. What is your passion?

> *"Do what you love, work really, really hard,*
> *be patient, be persistent, be open,*
> *work really, really hard some more,*
> *and the money will follow."*
> ~ Curt Rosengren ~

Where Do Great Ideas Come From?

Have you considered asking your staff? They often have good ideas but not always the outlet to provide them. Offer them a form to complete:

➢ Idea
➢ Cost
➢ Reasons why the plan may not work and solutions to those issues

Be sure to be open and really listen to their ideas. Acknowledge that their perspective and suggestions are important. Remember, you do not have to use the entire idea, maybe only just a portion. Some of the best ideas come from customers or employees.

Where do your great ideas come from?

Making the Staff Aware

By far the biggest complaint I hear from staff is, "No one ever tells us what is going on around here." As managers, you should take that as a challenge. Use every opportunity to share all aspects of your business. I understand that you cannot share information on personnel issues and payroll, but everything else of a non-confidential nature should be communal among the staff. Why are you keeping it from them? Shouldn't they be aware of what is going on?

Lack of communication can easily make the company look bad. For example: The Marketing Department does some great work—colorful coupons, slick brochures, and dynamic marketing ads. The customer cuts out the coupon and brings it to the business, only to be greeted with, "I didn't even know we had one of those," or "I don't know how to ring that up." Be sure that all employees are aware of marketing materials and how to handle coupons when received. Give them the information and make them responsible for reviewing the current promotions. You can post this information in employee rooms and/or by cash registers. Another method would be drafting a memo to explain the policy and process or cover the details at a staff meeting.

Communication is the role and responsibility of both the management team and the staff. There are just too many excuses for the breakdown in communication. Stop making excuses and find out better ways to communicate. As a manager, consider opening up the lines of communication yourself, and ask your staff what they would like to know about.

If at all possible, have weekly meetings to keep people informed. Those meetings are especially important when there are shift changes or from department to department.

And once the communication channels are open, keep them that way.

Surround Yourself with Great People

How much of your life have you spent in the company of negative people? Why? By choice or simple logistics? Assuming that *you* are not a negative person, I'm sure you've discovered what a difference it makes when you surround yourself with more upbeat people, those you truly enjoy being around.

As mentioned earlier (and I'm mentioning it again because it has such a horribly detrimental effect on employee morale and performance), negative people want you to come into their world...it's the old "misery loves company." Do not let them do this to you! Run as fast as you can! Otherwise you'll be audience to their constant litany of how they dislike their job, the company, their boss—how they're being overlooked or used as scapegoats—how the company is failing and all the customers are morons. That's ridiculous.

Your approach, if a hasty retreat would be too rude, could possibly be to hear them out only long enough to determine if any of their complaints are legitimate. If you think there is support for their constant grumbling, direct them to the Human Resource Department, or the proper person or channel that could help them. If *you* aren't the one with the authority to correct the situation, send them to the one who can. Otherwise, you'll continue to be a magnet for their repeated criticism.

On the other hand, if their complaints seem nothing more than a pity party, or they seem to be more the problem than the solution, you need to cut it short before the negativity becomes contagious. You can be sympathetic to the person's concerns while trying to put a positive spin on it—that perhaps he's not seeing the whole situation—or at least that *you* don't see it in the same way. If everything else fails, all you can do is remove yourself from it as gracefully as possible. Negativity is like a virus, and it can spread through the entire company.

So that being said, what people do we want around us? How about people who support us? How about people who have some of the same interests and outlooks on life? People who are part of the solutions, or at least willing to look for them, rather than being a big part of the problem?

What Can You Learn in an Hour?

A general manager of a local company that I consult for spends one hour each week working a different job within the company. He will work in accounting one week, marketing another week, in sales, in shipping, etc. He has found that in just one hour he can get a handle on what is going on in that department. And to make certain he accomplishes it, at the beginning of each month he calendars an hour a week or he would never find or make the time for it.

His employees seem happy that he is interested in getting to know their jobs and a little bit about them as people; and from his standpoint, he says that there is no better hour that he spends in any given week, encouraging those within departments to do the same. This all started when one of the managers overheard one department talking negatively about another. The manager knew that it was just a misunder-standing of what each department did and how their jobs fit into the big company picture. So he had them each spend an hour in the other department—he said it was like a miracle.

So, he took it a step further. He had the shifts trade places, working for only an hour on each other's shift. While there had previously been much discussion that different shifts didn't do this and didn't do that, there is now an understanding of what the various shifts are responsible for and their place in overall company performance.

Schedule an hour today. You will be happy that you did.

Accountability—Important For All

I was consulting for a company that was having trouble with accountability issues. People were not completing tasks, they were not coming in on time, and they were not living up to what was promised or expected. So, where does accountability begin? Like many other corporate elements, it begins at the top. Managers set the benchmark and serve as a role model.

Part of any manager's job is to provide his employees with the tools to succeed—not to set them up for failure. If goals aren't being met, if deadlines are missed, if performance is in any way falling short, it can often be a simple matter of unclear communication. Make certain that all job responsibilities are clearly understood, all project details and demands are known to those involved. Give your employees the tools to succeed, then hold them accountable.

I always recommend this—if you have accountability issues within the company, the manager should take a look at how he is managing his own accountability. Usually, the changes can begin there.

Train the Trainer to Train the Trainee

Many companies offer formal training programs, while others indoctrinate new staff through the more casual and often standard on-the-job training. The problem with informal (and even sometimes formal) training is that the trainers are often not trained to train. While that's not quite the tongue-twister or riddle that it seems to be, it can cause problems. For example:

A new employee is coming on board and a co-worker is assigned to train her. They are going along fine until the current employee mentions that she is going to show the trainee the way the company *wants* things done, as well as the way she should *really* do the task. The current employee begins introducing the trainee to other staff members; then after they are out of ear shot adds negative "insider" comments like, "Don't tell them anything" or "Be sure you watch your back with them."

A business acquaintance of mine worked an interim job for several months, a temporary position with a good company and seemingly good employees. Her biggest frustration with the job was that, even with 20 years' administrative experience, she was approached like a two-year old who knew little to nothing about standard office operations. Perhaps in their being eager to help, the employees innocently went a bit too far in their explanations. But coupled with this there were six long-term employees in the department; and within any given day's time she was "trained" in six different ways to do the same simple task. Obviously it wasn't a matter of protocol, but a matter of opinion. Realizing this, she kept quiet and simply juggled her work methods—finishing a task in any one of six different ways depending on who needed the work done.

How can you be assured that this does not go on at your company? The first and most important step is to select the correct trainer. The person should have a positive outlook and be very knowledgeable of the job as well as overall company policy. The guidelines should be clearly laid out for this person, including expectations. Also, make certain that adequate time is set aside for the training. Often training opportunities are rushed, and the employee is not provided ample time to take all necessary notes and absorb even a fraction of the information. Training can be overwhelming.

After a couple of weeks, a follow up should be done with the trainee to find out how well they were able to apply the material covered in their training. At that time, the trainee should be complimented (as appropriate) and corrected (as appropriate).

It is important to understand that what you train today is how your employee will work tomorrow. Set your training policies now.

Set a Company Code

Many companies have what is called a ten-foot rule. If employees come within ten feet of a customer, they are expected to acknowledge that customer. But, what if two employees are having a conversation and a customer approaches? A company code would go something like this:

If a customer comes within ten feet of any employee or group of employees, the conversation between employees should cease immediately. Remember, there is nothing more significant than the customer in front of them. Even if the conversation is an important, business-related discussion, it can be continued once the customer is assisted.

Another instance may be if a customer asks an employee for directions. A company code would go something like this:

If a customer asks you for directions, you are to take them to their destination. No pointing, no verbal directions, escort them.

What is your company code?

Staff Meetings

I know, we all hate them. Those boring, multi-hour meetings that really just go on and on and on. And you know that the feeling is rampant when you read studies and surveys with results showing that 25% of management would prefer going to the dentist rather than sitting through another meeting. If a root canal or extraction—the awful whine of the dentist drill—sounds like more fun than a staff meeting, something is very wrong.

If you're a manager and *you* hate them, imagine what your staff must think about them. If you add in the fact that the majority of managers may spend 30-60% of their time in meetings, they're not only *dreaded* events but very costly ones as well. To make the most of your company's time and money, remember these standard things when conducting the next meeting:

- ➤ Start and end the meeting on time.
- ➤ Always have an agenda that is passed out prior to the meeting, one which includes a timeline for every item and the person responsible.
- ➤ Focus on specific decisions, not long-winded discussions of unnecessary issues.

➢ Keep to the agenda and allow time at the end to go around the table to ask for a fifteen second update.

➢ Assign someone to take minutes and distribute the minutes within 24 hours of the meeting.

➢ Set ground rules to prevent people from hogging the meeting, saying inappropriate things, etc.

➢ Keep the meetings upbeat (when appropriate).

➢ Assign a chairperson to lead the meeting, following Roberts Rules of Order.

➢ Learn to say no—if you're continually asked to attend unnecessary meetings. Some things can be settled via phone call, through sub-committees, or informal discussion. Learn the difference.

Along the lines of that last item, consider a shorter meeting. How about a 90-second meeting, where everyone gathers, information is shared, and everyone moves on. How much can be exchanged in 90 seconds? A whole lot, if everyone comes prepared. Do not have people sit down, keep them standing. Give everyone a specific amount of seconds to share. Although 90 seconds might not be enough, think about the time needed and keep it brief. This will keep those who go on and on from going on and on.

Meetings are important—and a *well planned* meeting can be priceless.

Nip it Now

One of my favorite sayings comes from *The Andy Griffith Show*. Barney Fife always said, "Nip it, nip it in the bud." What does that have to do with business? Everything. Let's use this example. An employee comes in late and you do not address it. What do you think that tells the employees? It tells them that coming in late is acceptable. What if your policy is that all employees must wear nametags, every day, no exceptions, and an employee comes to work without their nametag? Do you send them home? You cannot afford not to. Because eventually what happens is that other employees will come in without their nametags. Then some will start coming in late and others will find still other rules to break. If the policies aren't adhered to and enforced, they will continue to be disregarded.

But I don't always blame the employee; sometimes it is the fault of the employer. Did the employer make the expectations clear? Was it clear what the consequences would be if the employee didn't wear his nametag? Did the employer follow up with the consequences?

Have you ever been in a situation where things just got out of hand? It may have started off small, and over time managed to grow to phenomenal and destructive proportions. In retrospect, don't you wish you would have just handled it when it started instead of letting it get to the level that it did? That is exactly what I am talking about when I encourage you to nip it in the bud.

I was at an event one time where an otherwise friendly person was somewhat cold to me. I could have left it at that, but I truly did not know what the problem could be. So I asked her if there was a problem and she said, "NO." Her tone of voice had me asking again, "Are you sure, because I feel like there is a problem between the two of us and I would like to resolve it." She said, "I don't have the problem, *you* have the problem."

When she went into greater detail I realized that I had forgotten to thank her for some volunteer work she had done. You see, I had thanked everyone but had forgotten to list her name. I apologized profusely, sent her a card, and followed up further with a telephone call. When she realized my sincerity, she put it behind her and we went back to the way things had always been between us.

What would have happened had I not nipped it? She would have remained upset and I would have thought, "I wonder what it is that she is upset about. It might have been the time that I ..."—then the speculation begins, and you can drive yourself crazy trying to figure out just what you might have done.

From an employee's side, there is a time that you should nip things in the bud. For example, what if an employee hears a rumor? Instead of talking about the rumor (which means you are actually continuing to spread the rumor), why not address it with the person who can factually answer the question.

When I deliver training, *nipping it in the bud* seems to be the most remembered item of them all—and I always encourage people to do just that whenever the situation warrants. Here are some examples:

A manager said to me "We have a problem with tardiness. All of our employees seem to come in late and it creates problems for our customers." I asked the manager why the employees continually came in late and he said, "I don't know." I can tell you why. It is because no one "nipped it in the bud." The first time an employee comes in late you cannot just let it go by, you have to acknowledge it in some way. It could be as subtle as you wish, but it must be acknowledged. The second time the employee comes in late, it must be addressed again. This time, you should remind the employee what time they are supposed to arrive at work. The progressive action from there should be a written warning if needed.

Let's say that you have had an employee working for you for five years and they have never had a tardiness problem and all of a sudden they have been tardy the last two days. Sit down and talk with them about it. Maybe they could use some assistance in some temporary flexible hours. If approached correctly, they will appreciate the intervention.

If Bob comes in late four days in a row, then Sally decides she can come in late because nothing happened to Bob, then Bill starts coming in late. Well, you get the point. Why do managers not want to deal with situations? Because they are uncomfortable. I can guarantee you that the situations are more uncomfortable when they go on and on. If you came in late every Friday for seven months and no one said anything to you, and all of sudden someone said, "I am writing you up for coming in late" what would you say? I must say that I have never looked back on a situation and said, "Man, I wish I had never nipped that in the bud."

☙

I spoke at a public seminar several years ago; and at its conclusion, as I always do, I stayed around to answer additional questions. A manager came up to me and said, "I have one of those employee problems you talked about. They come in late all of the time." I asked her how long this had been going on and she said, "two years." Two years? She went on to explain that her predecessor had never addressed the situation and it was a problem she had inherited. Well, there is a new sheriff in town. And the time has come. I explained that she should sit down with all of the staff, let them know the rules begin today, and that the line has been drawn in the sand...that from this day forward, all rules will be taken seriously. Please do not let your employees be late for two years. Remember to approach problems directly.

Barney Fife was no savant, but he sure knew what he was talking about on this one!

Employee Expectations

Make a list of the expectations you have for your employees. For example, the list could include wearing their nametag, following the dress code policy, being on time, coming to work as scheduled, greeting customers, etc. Review the information with every employee at their orientation, giving real examples. Then the employee should be asked to sign the paper and be given a copy for his own records. Items should be reviewed with all employees frequently. The signed commitment will help both parties understand the expectations. After all, employees cannot meet expectations they are not aware of and have not committed to.

You should also review the expectations periodically, making certain that *you* are exceeding them as well. The best model is a role model.

The Right Man ~ or Woman ~ for the Job

Think of your favorite baseball team. Every single time the closing pitcher is pulled in, he loads the bases and loses the game. But without fail, the coach continues to put the reliever in and the reliever loses the game. Isn't the coach just setting this pitcher up for failure? Isn't it clear that he cannot play under pressure?

Have you ever set any of your employees up for failure? Have you put them in a position that is not suited to their personality? Maybe you have someone as a front-line staff member who doesn't relate well with customers. Or maybe you have someone in sales who does not follow up well or lacks the confidence to promote the product. Have you ever moved an employee from one job to another because they have failed in every prior job and you were determined that they had to fit somewhere? Has that worked well for you?

It is just as important to understand what the employees can do well as it is to understand what they *cannot* do well. I have learned and have been shown repeatedly that a great manager hires and surrounds themselves with employees who enhance them. For example, if the manager excels at being a people person but is not very detail oriented, the best employee that she could hire is someone who is detail oriented. That way, all of the bases can be covered. Think of it as a spoke in a wheel. Which spokes are missing?

Help your staff find the position that is right for them.

> "Management is efficiency in climbing the ladder
> of success; leadership determines whether the
> ladder is leaning against the right wall."
> ~ Stephen R. Covey ~

Please...Hire Competent People

Not everyone is suited or trained to work in customer service. And apparently, not everyone is trained to give back change. My point:

My sister went into a local sandwich shop. She placed her order, paid for the order, then looked down at the receipt and noticed that she hadn't been given the discount on the sandwiches as it had been advertised. The employee attempted to subtract the amount, re-figure tax, etc., which took much longer than it should have. As my sister looked behind her, she saw that the line was getting longer and longer. It became clear that the employee was unable to calculate the difference. So my sister said, "Instead of going through all of this and holding up your line, the difference is about the cost of two sodas. You can just give me those and call it even." Simple enough, she thought. The employee went over, made two sodas, came back and said, "That will be $2.81." What? Attempting again to clarify the situation, she said, "I meant that we could just substitute the difference for these sodas." At which point he opened the cash drawer and gave her some change. She finally took the change and walked away discouraged. The employee never did get it.

Why would "counting change" not be part of the basic list of job skills? Yes, it's the millennium, and we know computers do the calculating for you—but sometimes the customer adds additional change after employees have entered the information into the computer. I have actually heard staff say, "I can't accept that money. Once I put it into the computer, I have to give you back what the computer says." Ugh. So, you have the perfect employee in all other respects, but they can't make change. Help them. Teach them. A good employee is constantly willing to learn.

A fully competent staff member will pay off for you in the long run.

Chapter Twelve

By the Book

Policies

Often we have "unwritten" policies that people just assume others will know. My question is, why not put these policies in writing? That way everyone is aware of expectations. Most "unwritten" policies are broken because they were never made clear to the employees to begin with.

Here are some ideas:

➢ Never speak negatively of co-workers, the company or your boss.

➢ Refrain from gossiping. There should be no tolerance for gossiping in your company. What good does gossiping do anyone?

➢ Acknowledge anyone who comes within ten feet of you, including your co-workers. (Staff need to be taught what type of acknowledgement is acceptable in your company.) Also, acknowledge everyone as they leave. Make it a customer service sandwich—get them coming in and going out.

➤ Thank everyone for coming in (at the end of their visit).

➤ Everyone must wash their hands after using the restroom.

You get the idea. Add to the list, make it business-appropriate based on your own company, and remember that if you're the boss you must abide by it too. If you do not, you are telling your employees that you either don't care or you're simply above the rules. If rules exist, they apply to everyone.

"The leader follows in front."
~ Proverb ~

Can you write a policy on negativity? You can if you are creative. One of your policies could be that employees must refrain from speaking negatively of their co-workers and your customers. What if a customer walked in to hear two of your workers speaking negatively of another customer? What should happen? If you have a policy in place, the answer to that would be clear.

Update your policies to keep everyone in the loop.

Dress Code

Yes, it deserves a section of its own. Wouldn't we all love to come to work in jeans? In sweats? In the most comfortable clothing we own? Over the last few years, companies who were previously "three piece suit" operations have relaxed to business casual. So, the trickle-down effect impacted those businesses that were previously *already* business casual and are now...well...*very* casual.

There are so many different views on this subject. Let's start with clean and pressed. That should be a given no matter where you work. We were in a restaurant and all of the waiters and waitresses were told to wear white cotton shirts, black slacks, and a name tag. There were six servers on the floor:

➤ Four had shirts that were wrinkled and looked like they had just been pulled from the dirty laundry
➤ Only two wore name tags
➤ Two had brown pants, not black

If they can't come to work at least looking clean and pressed, what do you do? Well, apparently the manager did nothing because these people were on the floor, serving his customers. Interestingly enough the manager said to someone, "I can't get my staff to come to work with clean and pressed attire." How about sending them home with no pay if they don't? It will happen only once. (By the way, that restaurant is no longer in business.)

Also, would you enjoy being served by someone who came to work in dirty, wrinkled clothes? Wouldn't you wonder about other things—like do they wash their hands consistently? Ugh.

Okay, so your company has a dress code. Business casual. Really, what is that? The clearer you are in your policy the less controversy you will have. Hint – if someone comes to an interview inappropriately dressed, you have your first clue.

When considering a dress code, consider your customers. One of our local tanning clubs has a very casual dress code. Many times the girls are in very short shorts and very revealing tops. Their thought is that they should be showing off their product—their tan. *My* thought is that they should be showing less of it. I'm not a customer there. The owner was born and raised in our community and realizes that people are very conservative. Even so, she wonders why her business has dropped by 20% since implementing the (lack of) dress code.

❧

We have a jewelry store nearby that has nice jewelry—clearly not high-end jewelry but you would never know that. Everyone dresses in very nice clothes and is always neat. Men wear ties, women wear stockings. People buy jewelry. The manager once told me that even though his jewelry isn't as high end as his competitor, he felt the need for his employees to dress and present themselves as if it were. By the way, his competitor went out of business last year.

Many fast food restaurants have adopted a dress code that now allows their employees to wear jeans. If you want to get an argument going in a training session, throw this one out: "My personal thought is no jeans." Oh man, is it ugly. I believe (and this is where the controversy comes in) that if you are in jeans, you are not at your peak performance. You are very casual and so is your work. (Feel free to become angry. It's okay.)

Like I mentioned before, I love jeans. They are very casual, comfortable, and are great for so many occasions. Okay, forget where you work. For the following professions, decide if you think jeans every day would be appropriate. Would you continue to see these professionals as professionals if they wore jeans? Remember, take yourself out of your profession:

➢ Doctors
➢ Lawyers

- ➢ Cooks
- ➢ Waitresses
- ➢ Retail Salespeople
- ➢ Bartenders
- ➢ Veterinarians
- ➢ Caterers
- ➢ Priests
- ➢ Nurses
- ➢ Plumbers
- ➢ Construction Workers

The other thing is—what are your competitors wearing? You always want to be a step up from them.

We have a local milk store in which the boys/men have to wear ties. Most of the employees are under twenty. In speaking with the manager, I asked about the ties, since the rest of the dress code is jeans. She said that boys who wear ties look nice. Period. If they are going to have to take the time to put on a tie, then they will take the time to present themselves well. It was only a few years ago that they allowed the employees to wear jeans. She has very strict rules on the jeans – they must appear ironed and must not have any holes. She also limits jewelry, etc.

Some companies have gone to uniforms, maybe something as simple as a pullover shirt with the company logo and the employee's name. As long as the uniform is appropriate for the environment, there is nothing wrong with this. The company should provide a week's supply of shirts for each employee. There should be a dress code policy in addition, that is very clear about expectations regarding cleanliness and upkeep, returning the uniform upon termination, etc.

How about an employee's overall appearance? How much is too much facial hair? How many are too many tattoos? Be sure that your policies are very clear on all issues to prevent any misunderstandings.

Enough about dress code, but I want you to take away at least one thing from all of this. Dress for your customers, not for the comfort of your employees.

Take Advantage of Technology But Do Not Get Lost in It

With today's internet, everyone is surfing the web. How is your website? You don't have one? Well, you need to get one. If you already have a site, is the information on the site easily accessible? Are your services clear? Do you keep the site updated? How does your site compare with your competitors' sites? If the information on your site is fresh and accurate, and provides the data people are looking for, it encourages them to visit more frequently. The initial money spent to build a site is worth every penny.

Those are the positive pieces of technology—but like everything else, there is a downside. The internet (versus personal service) prevents relationships from being built. There is a lot to be said for speaking with someone in person. Don't hide behind the computer. Even with e-commerce, you need to know that you are making first impressions online and should look for proper grammar, typographical errors, etc. Also, return your e-mails the same day. If someone sends you information, e-mail them back with a "thank you" so that they know you received it.

Take a look at your website!

Be Creative

One of my clients changed the ring tone of her office phone—it now rings with a chuckling laughter. She said that it helps her remember to always answer the phone with a smile. Another one of my clients has his phone ring to sound like a winning slot machine...it makes him smile and reminds him that every call is a potential new client (and sale).

I have investments with two local investment companies, both of which send me birthday cards each year. One of them sends a nice card signed by both the investment specialist and their assistant. The other is also signed by both, but always includes a short, personal note..."Dawn, hope you have a happy birthday. We really do appreciate your business. Enjoy a birthday ice cream on us. P.S. Tell your Mom I said 'hi'." They enclose a coupon for a free cone at the local dairy bar; and on our anniversary, Ted and I receive a card with *two* ice cream coupons. (Don't tell him, but I use both coupons myself.)

Working with the Media

Many companies use the local media, whether they place ads in the local newspaper or send press releases to the local television stations. So if everyone can do that, what are you doing differently? Instead of purchasing an ad that says "We have refrigerators this week for $399." How about placing a picture of a satisfied customer in the ad with a quote from them about service: "Sam and his staff went out of their way to assist us in finding the right refrigerator."

Maybe you have a chiropractic office. Why not write a weekly article for the local newspaper with tips and advan-

226 | Customer Service and Beyond

tages of chiropractic care? What a great way to help people and get your name (and website) out to the public. If you are a dentist, you could give dental hygiene tips or information on new procedures of benefit to the patient. The list is endless.

Get to know your local media.

Know Your Competitor

I can guarantee that the businesses leading your industry know everything about you. They visit your website frequently. They know what type of brochures you have available. They acquire any and all information they can about your company. Why? Because they want to know that they are keeping six steps ahead of you.

So, what can you do? All of the above. You should know what they are selling, how much they are selling it for, their hours, their largest clients, special promotions, etc. If a competitor in your field decided to build their business right next to you, what would you do? You would learn more about them. That is what I am saying. So, pretend their business is going in right next door to you tomorrow. What would you do? Be proactive. By doing so you'll have no need to be *re*active.

The Grass is Greener

In situations where there are multiple shifts, it is not uncommon to hear, "the *XYZ* shift doesn't do anything." It is amazing that people have preconceived ideas of what other people do (and don't do) on another shift, in another department, for another job. In most cases, the employees really have no idea at all. Without knowing the job, doing the job or at the very least seeing the work being accomplished, those comments are nothing more than unsupported opinion. If you are dealing with animosity between shifts, I recommend the following:

> ➤ Sit down with the leads on both shifts to discuss what staff is saying.
> ➤ Ask each shift to write down what they think the other shift does great and what they think the shift may improve on.
> ➤ Ask everyone to switch shifts at least once. This will help with perception issues.

Common comments from day shift staff:

"I sure wish I worked on the midnight shift. They don't do anything."

"They leave everything for us to do and never do anything at night."

"I'm not coming in for a meeting at 7:00 p.m. That is the time I spend with my family."

Common comment from the night shift staff:

"The day shift staff has no idea how hard it is to be out of the loop."

"Why are all meetings scheduled around the day staff?"

"I'm not coming in for a meeting at noon. After working all night, that's when I'm sleeping."

My mom used to work at a bowling alley, and each Thursday at noon she would go in to pick up her check. When she walked in, she would always notice the employees just standing around, relaxing, and talking to one another— never finding them the least bit busy or overworked. And yet when she came to work that night, she would often have notes that said, "We were swamped today and couldn't finish this or that." She became very frustrated with the situation.

When she told me this, I asked her to do me a favor. The next week that she went to the bowling alley to pick up her check, I asked her to go at 2:30 instead of noon. She didn't understand why, or at least I didn't think she did. She arrived at 2:30 p.m. as I had asked and sure enough, my phone rang at 2:35. She said, "I get it." Her perception had been that they didn't do anything during the day, but when she went at 2:30 p.m., everyone was hard at work. Why? Because she was going to pick up her check each week just as they were finishing their lunch.

Gaining perspective from both sides is the key, because then you have the ability to sit down and discuss the complete and actual issues. Remember, if you do not do something about it, it will not change.

Do You Really Care...

...or are you just going through the motions? A restaurant manager is walking around to the tables, visiting with the customers and asking if everything is okay. A table of four all had steaks. He asked how the steaks were. The first three people said "good" and the fourth person said, "it was okay." The manager moved on to the next table. What could he have done differently? Well, first of all, the manager should never have been satisfied with "it was okay." He should have asked if there was a problem, offered to have another steak prepared, comped a drink or dessert—anything to show that he was really listening and cared about the customer's experience.

If you are going to ask how things are going, be prepared to do whatever it takes for people to walk out saying that your company is "great." Don't settle for being mediocre.

> *"Customers don't expect you to be perfect.*
> *They do expect you to fix things*
> *when they go wrong."*
> ~ Donald Porter ~

Branding and Hooking

No, it is not what you think it is, but it sure did get your attention. Branding is an image that your company creates. For example, your letterhead, envelopes, thank you cards, brochures, newsletter, etc. all match. When someone sees your "look", they know it is your company. Hooking is your tag line or other hook that brings them in.

One company told me that their hook was cookies. (They sold office supplies.) They said that when they took the new brochure to their customers that they would also drop off homemade cookies. People would smell the aroma of cookies and would always associate the cookies with the office supply company. One particular company was an extremely loyal customer and ordered exclusively from them. About a year ago the office supply company began posting their catalogs online. The first thing that customer said was, "I guess that will be the end of our cookies." No way. The very inexpensive hook brought in a ton of money—and the hook continues today, with the delivery of the supplies.

Does your company have a branding? A hook? If not, you need one.

Who is Part of the Solution and Who is Part of the Problem?

I believe this: if you do not wish to be part of the solution then please do not be part of the problem. What do I mean by that? If you are an employee and you have a complaint with the company—about a policy, about anything—do not just voice the complaint but follow up with a solution. Here are some examples:

➢ Everyone should get a 10% raise this year.
➢ The sick policy is too strict.
➢ Let's open at 8:00 a.m. instead of 9:00 a.m.

I call those unsubstantial, whiney complaints. "The employees on the bus went whah whah whah!" Here are better ways for employees to approach these issues:

Everyone should get a 10% raise this year.

A 10% across the board raise would cost X amount of dollars. Those dollars can be earned through blah, blah and blah. Etc., etc.

The sick day policy is too strict.

If we were to revise the sick day policy to include all of the time (i.e. personal, vacation, sick) then people could use it as needed and would not feel the need to lie. Also, the time would be in their control and they would much more likely be discriminating about calling off at the last minute.

Let's open at 8:00 a.m. instead of 9:00 a.m.

We have heard from many customers (employee should attach comments) that they would prefer that we open a little earlier because they need to be at work at 9:00 a.m.

This would be a great interview question: "Give me an example of the last time you have been part of both the problem and the solution." So which are you? One of the problems or one of the solutions?

Downtime

Does your company have downtime? Or seasonal shifts in business? For example, after tax season, tax preparers aren't nearly as busy as during those frantic months when everyone's trying to beat the April 15 deadline. The same applies to restaurants during the hours of 2-4 p.m. Have you considered target marketing those who may wish to utilize your service (for a discount) during those off-times? A local restaurant offered discounts of up to 25% between the hours of 2-4 p.m. This held major attraction, especially to their senior population, and afternoon business increased 400%. Remember, those seniors tell their friends – and so on.

Downtime should also be used to prepare for those busier times ahead. There is *always* something to do. In any industry, cleaning and training are perfect fillers for downtime. In a restaurant, staff could also be stocking supplies, filling containers, cleaning, polishing, and sorting. At retail stores, staff can keep busy catching up on inventory, organizing, and refreshing displays. In offices, there's usually a to-do list a mile long not to mention the ever-constant filing. Staff who do not have anything assigned have a tendency to simply stand around. A very bad habit—and one that's easily begun

232 | Customer Service and Beyond

but hard to stop. Once staff members get in the routine of just standing around, they'll continue to do so whenever there's a lull in business. Should a customer walk in during that time, not only does it present a poor image of the company, but it is difficult for the employee to turn it around—to recharge mentally and get back in the work mode.

What do you have prepared for your employees during downtime?

What Should the Owner Do?

Let's start with the owner of a restaurant. Many managers feel the need to remain in the kitchen, overseeing the food preparation. As important as that is, a good kitchen manager can do the same thing. Where the manager should *really* be is serving as the host. There is no better opportunity to greet everyone who comes into their restaurant, have a nice conversation with them on the way to their table, check on them during the meal, and thank them for coming in. Unless you have an employee in mind who can WOW each and every person during every opportunity listed above, the person in that position has to be the owner. People *love* to meet the owner.

What if owners are not comfortable in this position? They should seek some training on how to do this right. The occasion serves as the perfect opportunity for them to learn firsthand how the customer's experience went, listen to any suggestions the customer has, and show their interest in the people who are supporting their business.

That all works well in a restaurant, but should a manager really act as a receptionist? Probably not. But if the hub of the office is on the third floor and the manager has an office by himself on the second floor, it just really doesn't make any sense.

The owner should have their hand on the pulse of the company. They should also spend time working at various positions within the company, not just sitting in an office. They should be out there, speaking with their customers at the customer's location. Don't just sit there. Manage by example.

Suggestion Box

Some companies embrace them. Other companies hate them. But, if questions are asked in the correct way, then it can be one of the best resources for companies to attain customer feedback. Some questionnaires are designed with a numeric scale, such as 1-5, but what does that really say? Okay, so I give the service for your company a 4 out of 5. What does that tell you? Even when the numbers are assigned poor, fair, good, excellent ratings, etc., it still leaves much unanswered. How about changing the questions to allow for increased individual customer input? For example:

- What was the best part of your experience?
- Where do you see that we can make improvements?
- Would you recommend our company to your friends? Please let us know why or why not.
- Did we exceed any expectations that you may have had prior to coming to our company? In what ways?

Those are very general questions, but think outside of the numbers game. What you are seeking is real information. If you want to continue using numbers, that is fine; just consider adding a comment column so that people can provide personal input.

The questionnaires can be made available at the end of their experience, the forms can be mailed to them or a telephone call can be made to follow up. Either way, employees should not have access in any way to these forms. The forms should be mailed directly to someone in a sealed envelope.

I once observed employees rooting through a suggestion box, pulling out anything negative regarding them. Of course, when management opened the box, they believed that everything was fine. What they didn't realize was that 90% of the questionnaires had been destroyed because they had negative comments about the staff.

If you feel comfortable with your customers, sit down with them and ask them how things are going. Ask them if they have any improvement ideas. Ask them if they recommend your business to their friends. They may tell you what you do not want to hear, but the truth is you really need to hear it. If you don't know it's broken, you can't fix it.

Also, consider a suggestion box for employee usage. Yes, recommendations from the staff. There have to be some ground rules though. Can they remain anonymous? If not, will the suggestion ever be held against them?

Notes

Chapter Thirteen

Ins and Outs

"If service is the rent you pay for your existence on this earth, are you behind in your rent?"
~ Robert G. Allen ~

Get Involved in the Community

Some of the most successful companies devote hours and hours to community involvement. They've learned that getting involved generates a huge degree of personal and professional accomplishment. Consider the benefits:

➢ Shows that your company cares
➢ Markets your business
➢ Allows your staff to learn about and become part of the community (even if they do not live there)
➢ Provides that initial introduction to the community so when they come to your business, it is not such a cold call
➢ Allows tons of relationship-building opportunities outside of the office
➢ Allows staff to wear their company shirts to events

> ➢ Provides opportunity for media attention
> ➢ Just makes you feel good

There are many ways to get involved. You can work with the local food pantry, school, chamber of commerce, churches, non-profit and civic organizations, etc. and find the best means for your company to give back.

Small Businesses

Small businesses have a disadvantage to the larger stores in many ways. But, we have found some unique ways to look at those "drawbacks" in a positive light:
> ➢ Closer parking
> ➢ Personal service (but you must live up to this)
> ➢ Often more specialized merchandise
>   Easier and quicker accessibility to products
> ➢ If you are a small business, what is your niche?

Whose Job is it, Anyway?

While dining out one evening, I noticed that there was a used napkin right in the middle of the floor. Many minutes went by as I observed four (4) of the staff walk right over the napkin, one of those employees being the owner. In growing disbelief, I watched as the fifth staff member walked by—but *finally*, he was the one who stooped and picked up the napkin. When I complimented him on taking care of it, he replied "That's my job. I'm the bus boy." But who was *really* responsible for picking up that napkin? Everyone who works there.

It is amazing to me that so many people buy into the "it-is-not-my-job" theory. In every position that I have held, the last line on my job description has always been "all other duties as assigned." Even without that line, had I worked at that restaurant, I would have picked up the napkin anyway. Why? Because it IS my job to keep the positive company image intact – and it is everyone else's job as well.

As an employer, why not test this out immediately. At the interview, consider laying a wadded up piece of paper on the floor so that when the interviewee walks in, they must either pick it up or step over it. You can always teach people to pick up trash but wouldn't it be better to hire someone who already knows how.

What other jobs fall into the "who's job is it" category? How about smiling? Yes, smiling. Some will argue that "it is the job of the person who initially answers the phone." But truth be told, everyone answers the telephone. With that said, is it then everyone's responsibility to smile? Who is responsible for marketing your business? The Marketing Department? Even if you *have* a Marketing Department, it is not solely their responsibility. For example:

You work for a company who produces widgets. While you are shopping at a local grocery store, someone asks about the new line of widgets. You have a couple choices in how to respond. You could encourage him to contact your Marketing Department, at which point the option of customer contact is totally out of your control. Or, you can explain the product to him, right there in the middle of the grocery store. Better still, what if you have a sample with you? Hand it to him, along with your business card.

I know that some of you are saying, "This is my personal time. I am not at work." But in the service industry, you are always at work.

Let's put it a different way. You are shopping at a grocery store and see your local pharmacist, with whom you have been doing business for over twenty years. As you pass the pharmacist you say, "Well hello, it is so great to see you. I need to bring my new prescription by sometime next week." His only response is, "Okay." What do you think? Is the pharmacist on duty? Is saying "hello" in public while *not* on duty in his job description?

Think about whose job it is – it is yours!

Frequently Asked Questions

Do you deal with frequently asked questions? What are your hours? Where are your restrooms? What does that cost? Do you have a trashcan? Instead of sighing when the customer asks, keep a list of those frequently asked questions and try to resolve them.

Here are some solutions:

FAQ: What are your hours? Make sure that the hours are clearly posted and also available on the website and any handouts.

FAQ: Where are your restrooms? Signs should be easily visible. If feasible, consider moving the signs so that they extend out from the door rather than being flat against the door surface itself.

FAQ: What does that cost? Be sure that all items are properly marked with their appropriate price.

FAQ: Do you have a trashcan? Make sure that there are plenty of trash cans.

Make a list of your top five questions and ask your staff to assist in resolving them.

Be Consistent

Consistency is the attraction for many companies, especially those with multiple locations. If you visit a chain restaurant and love their pancakes, you can visit that same restaurant in another state and assume that the pancakes will taste the same.

Customer service is no different. It should be consistent. Let's say you have four employees who will interact with a customer from the customer's very first impression to the last. The first three service providers are very good, but the last one is horrible. What will the customer remember? Or, what if the customer has received good service the last nine visits, but on the tenth the service was seriously lacking.

Putting staff expectations into place becomes vitally important. The problems begin when exceptions become routine. For example, a company chose to utilize a consistent greeting, "Welcome to XYZ Company. My name is Dawn, how can I serve you today?" The company put this greeting into place so that regardless of the company location being visited, the customer received the same consistent greeting.

An employee at one of the locations wanted to be different, so she greeted the customers by saying, "Good morning, my name is Dawn, may I help you?" Not at all a bad greeting, and it doesn't sound like much of a change, but it detracted from the whole idea of consistency. So, other employees saw the opportunity to change up their greeting as well. Before you knew it, everyone was using a different greeting, and of course there were those who decided that they just wouldn't greet anyone at all. Often times when staff react with an obvious disregard for the rules, there are other underlying issues. Attitude, anyone?

Think of it as Your Own

If the business that you work for was the business you *owned*, what would you do differently? Here are some thoughts:

➤ Really get to know the customers
➤ Figure out money-saving methods for the business
➤ Likewise, increase revenue for the business
➤ Treat employees and others with respect
➤ Constantly market the business
➤ Do whatever it takes to keep the customer coming back

The list is endless. Great employees think like business owners. Great business owners think like great business owners.

Hygiene

A massage—relaxing, breathtaking, and fabulous. You are lying there, in the moment, when your massage therapist enters the room. They lift up the blanket to cover you up and whoa...they have body odor. The entire hour you try to concentrate on the massage but the smell overwhelms you. You realize that prior to your visit, the massage therapist was apparently taking a smoke break, reeking of stale smoke as well. What if they also had onions for lunch? The entire experience is, well, ruined, but, did the massage therapist really do anything wrong? Are they any different from anyone else who has a job?

$$\psi$$

We were being seated in a local restaurant. As the hostess walked in front of us, we noticed this wrenching smell. Not quite knowing where it was coming from, we sat down. As the hostess walked by to seat the next group of people, we realized that the smell was coming from her. She kept walking by, seating people. The smell lent absolutely nothing to our meal—well, actually it did; but not in the positive sense.

Our question became "Why hasn't anyone she works with/for said anything?" There were two possibilities—either they didn't know how to diplomatically approach the subject or they didn't feel comfortable talking about it. Hygiene is sure not something that is comfortable to talk about, but it must be done. In most cases, the supervisor is the appropriate person to deal with this issue. A direct, quick, to-the-point conversation is the best. Expectations should be set and follow up should be done (if needed). (Of course, if you notice improvement, proper acknowledgement would be okay.) How might you begin a conversation of this magnitude?

"Sally, I need to discuss a sensitive issue with you," and go from there.

If you do not address this issue, you take the risk of customers not returning, co-workers taking it upon themselves to discuss this issue with the person (with the worker most likely becoming embarrassed) or others making fun of your staff member.

It is often assumed that poor hygiene is due to lack of care of one's self. Sometimes, though, there are other circumstances. Women going through the change may have an odor. Someone who has nowhere to live may not have the means to a daily shower. The trick is to find out how you as an employer can assist the situation and do so.

What if someone has bad breath? What about smelly feet, unclean hair or dirt under the fingernails? In all of these situations, they should be handled directly. You are doing your employee a disservice if you do not handle it.

So, you have handled it and you have not seen improvement. If you believe the employee is purposely not fixing the problem, that situation should be addressed differently than if you feel the employee is making an attempt. If the employee is clearly not making an effort, the issue then becomes a disciplinary one. A written warning should be issued and measurable objectives should be set. If you feel the person is trying (for example, they are clearly taking more showers but their clothes smell), you should address the issue again and give more direction. You may suggest they clean out their closet and wash all of their clothes, hang a deodorizer in the closet, etc.

A great way to justify dealing with the situation is ask yourself "if I were a customer, how would that person's poor hygiene make me feel?" What if your waiter had an open sore? Ugh.

❧

The trend today is hand washing. Thank goodness. You don't really think about hand washing until you see someone handling your food or someone touching you. What policy does your company have on hand washing? Would well-posted signs be enough of a reminder or does a written policy need to be made? This subject should be taken seriously.

Many healthcare organizations have strict policies on hand washing and the wearing of gloves. Fantastic. But what about those organizations that are not as strict – restaurants, offices, factories, etc. Germs can be spread there as well. Some companies have gone as far as to install motion detectors in the bathroom to see who is and who is not washing their hands when they leave. If you are in the restroom at the same time an employee is, and you notice that they do not wash their hands, do you say something? Do you set the example by always washing your hands?

Make a "To-Do" List

I was in line at a department store. The checker was waiting for me at the end and asked if I was ready to check out. I said, "That was nice of you to seek me out," and she responded with, "It's better than working off the stupid list they give us to do during down time." Okay, I wasn't ready for *that*. She pointed to the list that had three sections:
> If you have one minute you can …
> If you have five minutes you can …
> If you have ten minutes you can …

Basically, the company was providing the checkers with viable and productive options instead of just standing around. Consider putting together a similar short list for you and your staff. Then there will be no excuse for them to be aimlessly standing around. And if you should still occasionally find one of them with arms crossed and leaning against the wall, suggest he clean the bathroom or take out the trash.

I'll bet he will suddenly remember any number of things that need doing.

Have a "to-do" list ready for your staff and assist them in sticking to it.

But Where Should We Park?

Recently I visited a small antique shop in a downtown neighborhood. I had heard that they had some wonderful antiques and wanted to give them a shot. It took me fifteen minutes to find a parking place within four blocks. I trucked to the shop and looked around. The owner came over to talk with me, asking where I was from and how I had heard about their store. (Great.) I told her that a friend had recommended them and that I was really enjoying browsing, even though it had been tough finding a parking place. She said, "Yes, I am glad we get here early in the morning so that we can get a place right in front." Did she just say what I thought she said? Right in front? Who should be parking right in front?

So, if I wanted her to see it from a different perspective, I would tell her this: I was at the largest retailer in our town last week. They have told all of their employees that they can park up front. With as many employees as they have, the customers never have a chance of finding anything close. What do you think her reaction would have been? Coming from a different perspective, her answer would probably have been one of disapproval. If the shoe fits...

Always think from the minds of your customers. After all, they are why you are here.

Define a Good Company Picnic

Many companies set out to do the right thing. They put a lot of time and money into a company picnic, and still only a few employees show. Surveys have cited a variety of reasons why people do not attend, the most common reason being that they didn't want to go "to work" on their day off. Other reasons included that company events were boring, that the weather was always too hot, and that people didn't want to be with their co-workers unless they absolutely had to.

WOW. For something that the company intended as a perk for the employees, it sure didn't appear that way. So, what is a company to do? Cancel all future gatherings? Probably not—but here are things to consider:

➢ Form a committee (I know, I know, I hate committees too--but this is important) with a select group of energetic staff as well as some staff members who have seemed negative of the company picnic in the past.

➢ Supply the committee with a budget.

➢ Allow the committee to put together a survey, asking other staff what they would like to see at the picnic. Also, do not be afraid to ask people why they haven't come in the past.

➢ Let the committee put together a proposal, including the event date, time, location, activities, food, etc.

➢ Make sure that it is clear whether or not children are invited. If they are, be sure to have plenty of things for them to do.

➢ Talk up the event in the company.

➢ Award fantastic attendance prizes (including a day off, gift certificates, etc.).

➢ Ask for RSVPs so that people recognize the importance of the event.

➢ Provide a small token to all who attend (maybe a coolie cup with the company logo or something similar).

These committees work out best if every committee member has equal roles. For example, if a member of the management team serves on the committee, they should not have any more say than the others.

Take a look at your company events. Could they use some help?

Celebrate Success

What do you have to be proud of? Are your customers aware of your accomplishments? Why not use your success to your advantage? Have you recently held a toy drive? Or has one of your employees earned a civic award? If so, those clippings should be posted. This will make the employee proud and will also show that your company employees are dedicated citizens.

Do you have goals for your company? So, let's say you have the goals and have reached them. Did you do something special for the employees? After all, they were a part of reaching the goal. Let employees sign a poster showing they met the goal. Get each employee an inexpensive "Emmy Award" with the goal inscribed on it.

What have you done to help your company celebrate success?

Business Mottos – If You Have One, Live Up to it

Does your company have a motto? Be careful with this one. Don't promise the impossible or exceedingly difficult. For example, "We are better than everyone else" or "We are friendlier than any other gas station." These mottos are fine, except how do you measure them—and are your employees aware of what it will take to reach these lofty goals?

I know one company whose motto is "Shop with us, where we go beyond in everything we do." Really? Because if they tell me that, then I am going to be expecting nothing less—watching every single move that they make and setting expectations higher than they can imagine.

Business mottos can be an effective tool, but just make sure that every single employee understands what it takes to successfully reach that goal. Am I saying not to set a hefty motto? Absolutely not. Here is an example:

If your motto is "shop with us, where we go beyond in everything we do," then you must:

➤ Exceed the customer's expectations 100% of the time. This means everyone from the front desk to the president to the salesperson to the overnight staff.

➤ Do everything better than your competitor. For this, you need to know what they are doing, how they are doing it, what works and what doesn't, and what it will take to do it that much better.

Can you think of others? Look at your business motto (create one if you do not have one) and make sure there are measurable expectations for your staff. Provide them with examples, role play the expectations, and help them along. Most importantly, set a good example.

Show Support

Support your local high school by posting their colors and other information such as uniforms, program books, sports and academic accomplishments, etc. People love working with companies that support their local students and schools.

If your customers have information in the newspapers such as birth announcements and newborn pictures, engagement photos, wedding and anniversary announcements, etc., post those for the public to view.

People will remember your community support.

E-Mail – Friend or Foe

"In the world of Internet Customer Service,
it's important to remember
your competitor is only one mouse click away."
~ Doug Warner~

Do you want to remind your clients about an upcoming event? Have you considered using e-mail? E-mail laws require that you first acquire their permission, accomplished easily by a simple signed paper. After you receive permission (and agree not to share their e-mail address with anyone outside your company) you can send them appropriate e-mails. You want to be careful on frequency and contents.

You can reach many people with one click of the button. Have you considered it for your business?

Point of Sale

We have all heard about the "point of sale" but what does that really mean? Well, plainly, it is the idea that while you have people at your business, they see something that they hadn't intended to buy but end up buying it anyway. Probably the biggest point of sale used would be those at the grocery store. You went in to buy a gallon of milk and ended up spending $25 on additional items (just because you saw them).

If you are in retail and advertise in the local newspaper or in magazines, have those advertisements posted at the entrance. If you have multiple page ads, make sure to have them available for people to pick up. Go a step further and include the location of the item (i.e. aisle 5). This is a simple yet very proactive way to assist the customer. Some may say, "if they have to look for the item, maybe we will sell other items too based on simple visual notice." I would answer, "if you provide this convenience for the customer, they will feel as if you have gone above and beyond for them. It will also help your staff from being bombarded with questions about the location of items. Your staff can concentrate on serving the customer in other ways."

How about this? If you own or manage a grocery store, have a nice display of items needed to make a particular recipe and have a copy of the recipe available as well. You can have all of the ingredient items readily available for someone to pick up. A one-stop shopping, if you may.

Marketing

What marketing products do you use to promote your company? We have seen the obvious—coolie cups, t-shirts, hats, pens, but let your creativity flow. A quilt shop owner purchased quilting finger cushions with her name and number on them. Every time the quilter made a stitch, she saw the quilt shop information. A local bakery personalized coffee cups for the *regulars*. They kept the cups and washed them and had them ready in the morning for their regulars. Less frequent customers saw the coffee cups, asked about them, then became regulars themselves. Those regulars pay your electric bill!

A local potato chip company was handing out chip clips. Attached to the chip clip was a warning: "When used with products other than ours, we cannot be responsible for contents."

People who refer others to you should be given incentives. For example, if someone makes a referral to you, in addition to a handwritten card (see Chapter Six) you should offer them a discount for sending you a certain amount of clients. Regardless of the business, we can all use extra marketing assistance.

Some companies try to market their business *within* their own business. One pet peeve I have is when businesses hang signs with exposed tape across the top. It looks tacky. Top it off with a typographical error and you have really annoyed me. Or a handwritten sign registers within the tacky caliber too. Do not even get me started on those. If you absolutely must tape up the sign, roll the tape behind the paper, please.

But a better idea would be to use a nice ($1) frame. It looks professional and can easily be changed out.

❧

I was in the waiting room of a very plush law firm and, as I often do, I was scanning the room. They had very expensive artwork, properly potted plants, framed awards, and *a handwritten sign*—taped to the door stating, "This door doesn't close by itself. Close when you come through." That single, taped up, handwritten sign took away from everything else in the room. Tacky.

❧

The trick to marketing is consistency. Your larger (and successful) corporations are very particular about color and content. Once your branding is established, be sure that it is utilized on every piece of marketing that goes out. That includes brochures, flyers, billboards, telephone book advertisements, websites, letterhead, etc. You will know your branding is successful when someone looks at it and immediately knows your company and what you do.

What does your branding say about your company? Does it say service? Does it say fun? Does it say professional? If you haven't revised your branding in a while (or have no branding), you may wish to consult with someone.

Take a look at one of the pens you have. Does it have a bank's name on it? You realize that every time you use that pen, you are marketing for that organization. Are they paying you to do that? Absolutely not, they are simply providing the tools for you to advertise for them. What items do you currently have or readily obtain that you could provide for people to market your business? Here are some ideas:

- ➢ Band Aid® dispenser from a healthcare organization
- ➢ Flashlight from a car maintenance garage
- ➢ Coffee cup from the local diner (encourage inexpensive refills)
- ➢ Individual moist towelettes from a restaurant
- ➢ Toothbrushes from dentists
- ➢ Chip clip from potato chip vendor
- ➢ Brush from hair dresser
- ➢ Eye glass cleaner from optometrist
- ➢ Magnet with important numbers from just about any business

Remember, people are forming a first impression, deciding if they will stop or not. Be aware of grammatical errors by double checking your signs, brochures, letters, etc.

Notes

Chapter Fourteen

Environmental Activists

No, we won't be discussing Greenpeace or Save the Rainforest, even though their concept is a noble one. But if we could just apply the same attitude and philosophy of those environmentalists to the workplace, we'd have an easy definition of concern for and improvement of our own business environs.

And there's no better place to start than ...

The Restroom

Yes, it deserves and receives a section all by itself. Justified or not, most people believe that the cleanliness of the restroom represents how the company operates. Even so, for many businesses restrooms appear to be the lowest priority—and boy do I have some stories for you.

One time we went to a store that actually posted the cleaning schedule on the wall. We were there on a Thursday morning at 10:10 a.m., and the checklist indicated that the

254 | Customer Service and Beyond

restroom had been cleaned at 9:00 a.m., 10:00 a.m., 11:00 a.m., and noon. That's interesting. Again, it was only 10:10 a.m. By looking around, it was obvious that the restroom had not been attended to in quite a while. Many stalls were out of paper and there was no soap in two out of three dispensers.

Why do people not take care of their restrooms? Or perhaps better put, why is cleaning the bathroom so hated? Do they see it as a degrading job—the task that no one wants to do—one that's sometimes used as "punishment" for the lowest ranking employee? Is it only the responsibility of the nighttime janitorial crew? No, it is everyone's responsibility. One of the most disgusting things that I have ever seen was the results of someone getting sick on the floor, all the way from the bathroom door to the stall. After seeing what had happened, I alerted an employee, who then alerted the manager. The manager's response to me was, "Our janitor doesn't come in until after we close" and then he walked away. So what he was really telling me was, "We don't care." I once overheard one employee telling another, "I'm glad we have our own bathrooms and do not have to use the ones that the public uses." Ugh!

❈

While we were waiting for a table at a chain restaurant, I visited the restroom; and I was washing my hands when I noticed two employees come in. There was toilet paper scattered on the floor, but they both walked right past it. Still, that was nothing compared to when they exited the stalls and returned to the dining room. Yes, you guessed it—they did not wash their hands. And how about *this* coincidence? Who was our waitress? You guessed it—one of those who did not wash her hands. I had a bad feeling in my stomach during the entire dinner and could barely eat. But at least we didn't have to worry about a repeat performance since we never returned to that restaurant.

Here is a simple checklist for your bathroom:

- ➢ Plenty of extra toilet paper and paper towels.
- ➢ Clean sinks, which would mean no mildew or water stains.
- ➢ Clean faucet, with no hard water buildup around the fixtures.
- ➢ Clean toilets, clean seat, and clean under the rim. The back of the toilet should be wiped down and even inside, where the toilet ball is.
- ➢ Room air freshener, either an automatic timer or an available can.
- ➢ Sign noting who needs to be contacted if there are any problems.
- ➢ Checklist (does not necessarily need to be visible) noting who is responsible and who cleaned last.
- ➢ Staff should understand that they are responsible for maintaining the bathroom each and every time they are in there.

Do you want to take your bathroom a step further?

- ➢ Fresh flowers (even two daisies in a small vase adds freshness)
- ➢ Toilet seat protective covers
- ➢ Baby changing space (that is wiped down daily)
- ➢ Great smelling soap options (as well as non-smelling soaps)
- ➢ Facial tissues
- ➢ Space for women to apply makeup

- ➢ Personal hygiene products
- ➢ Lotion choices
- ➢ Basket of personal products including hairspray, lotions, etc.

So, how does your bathroom measure up? Take a look around, then get busy. You don't want to end up as one of my stories.

Have Some Fun

Life is too short not to have a little fun, and yet still remain professional. We wanted to take a short vacation but couldn't decide where to go, so we paid a visit to a local travel agency. As we opened the door, we heard tropical music playing. There were leis hanging from the ceiling, grass skirts wrapped around the receptionist desk, coconuts on the floor, and fresh pineapple displayed on the counter. All of the staff were dressed in their tropical shirts, wearing nametags made out of plastic fruit.

As we walked in, the receptionist said, "Aloha, and welcome to the XYZ Travel Agency. Where may we send you today?" WOW! Who needs to book an exotic vacation when you can come *here*?

Everyone was so happy, smiling and waving at us from their desk. They all just seemed truly delighted to be working there. Who wouldn't? The receptionist went on to tell us that they were promoting their getaway vacations. Did I mention that it was the dead of winter and there was snow on the ground and the temperatures were in the twenties?

You guessed it. We booked a trip to the Dominican Republic. When I stopped by to pick up the tickets, they wished us well on our trip and provided us with a goodie bag of travel size items—tanning lotion, sunglasses, and some can coolies with their logo.

When we arrived back home again following a fabulous vacation, we had a card waiting for us in the mail. The card welcomed us home and included two coupons for free coffee at the local coffee house...saying that after all of the time away they knew we would have some trouble getting up our first day back.

Yes, we know you can book your travel online and probably save a little bit of money; but for us, the **total experience** of this transaction was worth any amount of money we could have saved.

Think about your office—would it ever be appropriate to decorate to celebrate a special event? How can you provide an environment for your staff to have fun (yet be professional)? Design your environment with your culture in mind and stay *active* in caring for it.

Preventive Maintenance – Don't Live Without It

A restaurant owner once said to me, "It seems like I do a terrible job with preventive maintenance. The same problems arise over and over again." For successful preventive maintenance, you need a good, written plan. I asked him to give me a list of three fires that he was continually fighting to put out. Here is what he came up with:

> ➤ *We always run out of toilet paper during the busiest time of the day.* Then, you should have plenty of toilet paper available at all times.

> ➤ *My cashiers need to change shifts and we have
> to close a line for ten (10) minutes.* Then you
> should have two drawers ready.
> ➤ *On Saturday afternoon we always run out of
> quarters.* Then you should make sure you go to
> the bank on Saturday morning to get plenty of
> quarters.

What would your recommendations be? How could the
company be more proactive? Do you have consistent fires?
What needs to be done?

Signs

Signs meant to be helpful sometimes create a negative
reaction—like the ones below. But with a little thought, you
can put a more positive spin on them:

> ➤ *The restroom is broke* ~ vs. ~ We apologize for
> any inconvenience but (state problem). Please
> use the facility down the hall.
> ➤ *Keeping your patience will help keep our
> patients* ~ vs. ~ We appreciate your patience.
> ➤ *No parking* ~ vs. ~ Thou shalt not park here.
> (Sign at church)
> ➤ *Glad you chose us over our competitor* ~ vs. ~
> You had a choice and you chose us. Thank you.

If you have lighted signs, make certain that:

> ➤ The sign can be seen from the road
> ➤ All of the light bulbs are working
> ➤ The area around the sign is clean
> ➤ The logo, phone number, and website are on the
> sign

> ➤ Landscaping around the sign is maintained

*Sign, sign, everywhere a sign, blockin' out the scenery, breakin' my...*Oops. Sorry. I'm having an accidental Five Man Electrical Band moment here and I lost my train of thought. Let's see, what I meant to say was please keep your signs maintained. You never know who might be reading them.

You're singing along, aren't you?

What is Too Clean?

Have you ever walked into a business and thought to yourself, "This place is just way too clean?" Probably not. So, the benchmark for your company is to keep it so clean that people could say that. But your company is a vehicle servicing company? Or a manufacturing plant? It doesn't matter. Common work areas, desks, receptionist areas, restrooms, company transport vehicles, and all other areas of the workplace should be clean and organized. You are making an impression.

I had an appointment to have new tires put on my car. When I walked into the office of this company, there was stuff stacked everywhere and everything seemed to have smudges of oil on it. It was fairly apparent that the office had not been cleaned out in years. They couldn't find a pen had their life depended on it. I know what you are thinking—"But it was a garage." Yes, it was. But their competitor, right down the street, has a nice clean waiting area, the office is very organized, and people know exactly where things are. Who would you rather do business with?

What can you do to clean up or de-clutter your workspace? Then keep it that way.

Why Do Your Company Vehicles Need Cleaning?

What's your impression of a business when their company vehicles pass you in traffic and they look like they haven't been washed in years? Or, what if you had the chance to peek into a company vehicle and there were empty fast food bags and other trash scattered throughout? You'd probably be grateful that you were only *looking*, not riding inside. But you'd also probably think that if they can't take care of their own vehicle, how are they going to take care of your service need.

Be sure to maintain the vehicles as if they are new, right off the lot. If necessary, put together a cleaning schedule for the staff to assist in keeping the vehicle maintained. Involve them all—the responsibility is shared by everyone.

When Do You Really Open?

I was sitting in my comfortable pedicure chair when the owner answered the phone. I heard him say, "We understand your work schedule is crazy and would be more than happy to see you at 9:30 a.m." I looked at the hours on the wall and noticed that they really didn't open until 10:00 a.m. I told the owner that I thought it was great that he was so accommodating to his customers, and he said, "The worst thing I can do is make them work around my hours, then have to go somewhere else, and like it better. Then I lose a customer because I wasn't flexible." Great point. Win-win situation.

Are you flexible with your customers? Are your hours meeting their needs?

Be Aware of Your Surroundings

Who is at your business? Who is in the restroom? Who is still on hold? I remember being in a small boutique for fifteen minutes before checking out. When I approached the counter, the clerk said, "I didn't even hear you come in." Heck, I could have robbed her blind, and she would never have known it (but she wasn't the owner so it probably didn't matter to her). Also, by not realizing I was there, she missed the opportunity to provide excellent service and possibly even upsell for the company.

There are so many things that can come into play involving people in your surroundings—safety—security-- service. How embarrassing to lock up your business with a customer still in the bathroom! But it *has* happened. It's also important to not only know who is there and where they are, but whether or not they have been helped. I never mind three salespeople approaching me at different times to make sure that I have been assisted. I would rather have *that* than not being able to find anyone to assist if and when I need it.

Remember to have one eye on your work and the other eye on people who are in your business.

The Waiting Game

Statistics show that a person waits (should we read that wastes?) an average of a year's time throughout his entire lifetime. Kind of makes you want to ask for a do-over, doesn't it? When is the last time you had to wait? At the bank? In the doctor's office? While stuck in traffic? If you are like me, you do not enjoy waiting; so what can be done to help make the experience seem shorter?

Let's look at the stuck-in-traffic experience. To pass the time, we play the radio, talk on the cell phone, listen to books on tape, or (if we have them) talk with other passengers in the car. Now, how about the doctor's office? We sit in uncomfortable chairs, read through the outdated and torn magazines, flip through the informational pamphlets that have nothing to do with us, and stare at the blank walls. What else could make this experience seem like less of a wait? How about a television set? The T.V. could run local stations—or how about a marketing tape regarding their practice? It could play a tape explaining the additional services that the doctor provides (a form of upselling, if you may) or it could run health trivia questions.

How long do you wait in a doctor's exam room? It would seem to be less if there were something to read. Remember...a wait is still a wait regardless of the length, and often the patient is nervous about the outcome of the appointment. Anything to help and distract would be appreciated.

"I took a course in speed waiting.
Now I can wait an hour in only ten minutes."
~ Steven Wright ~

Now, think about *your* business. Take a look at your waiting room. Better yet, *sit* in your waiting room. Be your own customer, and take a look around to see what there is to help pass time and perhaps market your business? Are your magazines up to date? (They should be no more than three months old.) Are there items for children—crayons coloring books, toys? (Even if children are not your direct customers, their parents are.) What about a daily newspaper? A daily newspaper says "we care."

How is the waiting room decorated? Have you used the opportunity to market yourself by displaying your mission statement, letters of acknowledgement, etc. on the wall? (Be sure that your mission statement is tangible and not just words.) Is the area clean and free of cobwebs and dust bunnies (or in some cases dust iguanas)? My advice would be to bring in professional cleaners no less than quarterly. *You* see this room every day. The professionals will be able to quickly pick up on the areas that need special attention.

Is the trash emptied every night? Is the trash bag changed as well? Would it be appropriate to offer a refreshment section? (I know what you are thinking—it would be messy. But remember, your goal is to be the best!)

The chairs in the room should be comfortable and accommodating for all. I am not a small woman. If all of the chairs have arms, sometimes I am not comfortable in them. Some chairs should have no arms, some should, some chairs should be made for children, etc.

When you design the waiting room, keep your culture and your customers in mind. There was a dentist's office that set a peaceful mood with tropical plants, soothing fountains, soothing background music, and beautiful scenic pictures. When I asked the staff about the decorating, they said it was the dentist's idea. He wanted to convey a serene environment because no one likes going to the dentist. People are already anxious when they arrive at the dentist's office. So if they are soothed a bit in the waiting room, they are less nervous in the dentist's chair, which proves to be a better experience. My dentist now has a television hanging on the ceiling for me to watch while I am in the chair. I even get to hold the remote!

Can't think of anything that you can do to improve your customer's wait? Calculate the average wait of your customers and then sit in your waiting room for that same length of time. Consider how frustrating it is to wait. If you can make the wait seem a little shorter for the customer, their overall experience will be improved as will their impression of your business.

Cleanliness—The Essentials

Basic cleaning is within everyone's job description, and it is the manager's responsibility to make sure that everyone understands that. How can they do that? To begin, the manager needs to set a good example. If the manager sees trash on the floor, he can pick it up as easily as anyone else. If someone spills a drink, get a rag. I am not saying that the manager is the janitor. I *am* saying though that he needs to set a good example, and he's not above doing anything he'd ask of his employees. If it needs done, just do it. And that applies to everyone.

Beyond the restrooms, there are entryways, meeting rooms, kitchens, offices, and so many more places where dirt loves to hide and accumulate. But who cleans it up? For those large cleaning projects, have a specific schedule. "There is dust on the lights so it must be time to dust" does *not* qualify as a schedule. Sit down with your staff to obtain their ideas on how best to keep your workplace clean. Having a plan is a great start, but if it needs cleaned now, *it needs cleaned now.*

How clean is your business? Have the trash cans been washed out recently? Is there dust in the light fixtures? Is your entrance full of dirt? Sometimes it is very difficult for people to assess the cleanliness of their own business. Go to the front door and walk in as a customer. Look for areas that need attention. Remember, the person who visits your business for the first time will see it from a new perspective. You should try to see it before they do.

You may be able to do the cleaning, or at least some of it, in-house—but it may be a better idea to bring in an outside service. Lay out specific expectations for the company. As for your own staff, my philosophy has always been that every employee should "clean mean and mean to clean." Are you setting a good example?

Display Ways Your Business Can Help

I was seeking a new look for my bedroom but had no idea of what I was really looking for. When I walked into the store, I immediately saw a bedding display that knocked my socks off. It was perfect. There were pillowcases, sheets, shams, and a comforter in the ideal pattern and color, showcased in a display that begged me to take it home. I spoke with the salesclerk about purchasing the entire ensemble. But when she brought me the package, I barely recognized it. The photo on the outside of the packaging didn't do it justice at all, and I would have never purchased it had I not seen it displayed.

How many of you have ever gone to the grocery store and thought, "What should I cook for dinner?" How about this – the grocery store displaying a complete meal... and next to the display they could have a recipe card and all of the supplies which are needed. It doesn't get much better than that. To take it one step further – have someone handing out samples.

Another successful way to show people you can help is to show "before" and "after" pictures. This would work for an automobile detail shop, a beauty shop, and even a nail shop. But what would work for you?

Many financial institutions have much to offer, many items of which we are never made aware of. For example, many of them now have health savings accounts. (Check with your financial institution.) If they have this available, they should use every opportunity to promote it. Flyers and posters are fine, but wouldn't an employee talking about it be the best display ever?

What if you sold vinegar? How many ways can you it – for salads, cooking, marinating; to clean bathrooms, dishwashers, coffeepots, and windows; to ease sunburn, bee stings, hiccups—the list goes on forever. So why not display a bottle of vinegar and show all the ways in which it can be used?

What can your business display?

You Always Represent Your Company

We were building a house, and my husband wanted me to find the contact number for a certain window company that had been highly recommended to him. On that day, I happened to be in traffic behind a truck with their company logo on the back. I quickly grabbed a piece of paper and wrote down their number...just in time, as I had to pull into the left lane to make a turn. In three lanes of traffic, I was all of the way to the left, the company truck was in the center, with a small car in the right lane. I couldn't believe it when the driver of the company truck gave the small car the finger. I didn't know the cause, but it doesn't really matter what that car or driver did; the truck driver is still representing the company.

They may have been well recommended to *us*, but they certainly didn't recommend *themselves* well at all—and we gave the job to another company. Remember, when you wear your company shirt or drive your company van, you need to be aware that you are representing the company. You *are* the company in the eyes of whomever sees you. You are always representing your company, whether you're "in uniform" or not. I know what you are thinking. "But they don't pay me to represent them 24/7." Well, maybe you do not receive a paycheck for all 24 hours, but you should understand that people are always drawing an impression.

> *"As far as customers are concerned you are the company. This is not a burden, but the core of your job. You hold in your hands the power to keep customers coming back – perhaps even to make or break the company."*
> ~ Anonymous ~

I'll give you a great example. We had just moved to Troy a few months prior, and I really did not know a lot of people. I started my job with the Chamber on a Wednesday. On Saturday morning my favorite thing to do was to put on a pair of sweats, a t-shirt, no makeup (no need to envision that), pull my hair back, and head to the grocery story. It was just nice to not have to get dressed up to go out. So, as I am strolling through the grocery story, a gentleman in a suit steps up to me and says, "Are you Dawn Mushill, the new Director of the Chamber?" I froze. I said, "Yes, I am." He put out his hand and said, "I am State Representative Ron Stephens. Your office is in my building. Welcome to Troy." Oh man, was my face red. I had made a first impression alright, and I've tried my best to forget it ever since. I tell that story in many of my trainings and each time I tell it, I have that same sinking feeling in my gut.

When I am at a Chamber event, representing the Chamber, I feel the need to refrain from drinking alcohol. I am wearing a Chamber shirt with my name on it and I need to have a clear head; and so many years ago I just decided to not drink alcohol. At an event a few months ago two gentlemen approached me with a beer and said, "How about a beer?" I pointed to the name on my shirt and said, "I'm sorry, I do not drink with my shirt on." You guessed it. They did not pass up the opportunity—"Well, do you drink with your shirt off?" Okay then.

Remember, you are representing your business all of the time.

Notes

Chapter Fifteen

The Customer

"The customer is our reason for being here."
~ Anonymous ~

Who is your customer, really? What do you know about them? Why did they choose *your* company over another company? Do they have preferences? Were they referred? The best way to really get to know your customer is to listen to what they have to say. Pay attention Be interested. If appropriate for the customer relationship, get to know about their family. Their preferences. Anything that makes them unique. Build a relationship that will last for a long time and keep them coming back.

The Revolving Door

It's always good to see a friendly face; and when a customer brings repeat business to our company, it feels like we should lay out the red carpet for them. But if a red carpet isn't handy, or would be way too over the top, what should we do? Here are some things that will let them know that you are glad to see them back—and that they will receive the same great service that impressed them the first time:

- ➤ Welcome them back (as opposed to just saying "hi") and call them by their name if possible.
- ➤ Discuss the reason they were at your business in the first place. For example, "How did that red sweater work for you last time?" or "I remember when you were leaving here last time your niece was getting married. How was the wedding?" or "Did your homemade tacos turn out well?" Remembering this information says so much. It lets them know that you were listening the last time you saw them and that it meant enough for you to remember. (If you have a rotten memory, make certain you have an amazing Rolodex or customer file. Keep a list of customers and subjects that you discuss, so that the next time they visit you can refer to your notes.)
- ➤ Thank them for coming and let them know you hope to see them back soon.

What is your revolving door?

Be a Good Customer

I love those moments when I deliver customer service training and the customer service representatives say, "Can you give training to our *customers*?" Unfortunately I have to say, "No, I can't. But I *can* help you deal with poor customers." And inevitably the conversation turns to the top three things that drive customer service representatives crazy:

> ➤ Customers who are using cell phones (or cell phone ear pieces) during a transaction
> ➤ Customers who do not listen
> ➤ Customers who look down on the customer service staff

Then I say "Have you ever done any of these things yourself?" Usually everyone raises their hand. My point is: The way a customer acts often depends on how a customer service representative *reacts*.

Here are some thoughts:

> ➤ Address problems with the appropriate people immediately. If you have an issue about a company, ask to speak with a manager. Although the front-line staff would probably listen to you, it isn't likely that they are empowered to make all authoritative decisions. When speaking to the manager, lay out the scenario quickly, and without emotion. Provide the facts of the situation.
> ➤ Use good manners. You should look service staff in the eye, smiling, and acknowledging their presence. Too many people look down on workers in the service industry and then ask why there are no good service people.
> ➤ Treat the service staff like you would like to be treated. It is cliché, I know--but still true. If you were the service provider and the customer had a problem, how would you like to be approached?

There are so many things that come into play with any customer encounter – body language, eye contact, first impressions, the handshake (when appropriate), surroundings—and so much of it is overlooked. Everyone has an opportunity to make the *visit* more than just a visit—to make it an "experience."

If you visit a grocery store, and the only thing the checker asks for is your money, she has missed the opportunity to offer you an experience. Let's *create* an experience... one I would envision at a grocery store checkout line.

As you enter the store, the first employee you come into contact with actually acknowledges you. The store advertisements are neatly stacked and readily available. The carts are free of trash and any remnants of whatever weather may be occurring at the time. While you walk through the store, the floors are clean, the produce is fresh, the shelves are well stocked, and the staff is friendly. At the end of your market adventure, you begin placing your items on the checkout roller and the checker acknowledges you with a smile. Before she begins scanning your order, she says, "Hello, how are you today?" while making direct eye contact. Once the checker begins scanning, she also begins the conversation, maybe about an item, acknowledging something that is on sale, or maybe talking about a recipe. The idea is that you want this to be an experience. The conversation is focused on the customer and not with another employee.

As the checker finalizes the order, she lets you know the total rather than simply expecting you to read the computer screen. She will verify the amount you give her ("that will be XX out of $20"). Not only is it an added courtesy, but repeating the amounts also helps in reducing error. And goodness knows, those are easy enough to happen at *any* register. (A friend told me that just recently her bank failed to give her the cash back from a deposited check—twice—and these are the people who are handling her money?)

Once the transaction is complete, the checker should thank you for choosing their particular store and say, "We hope to see you soon." If it appears as if you may need some assistance to your car, it should be offered—and if it is raining, the cart clerk should offer to walk you to your car with a store's umbrella.

Wow. If a grocery store could consistently provide each and every customer this level of service, the store would be packed each and every day. People would shop there simply for the exceedingly excellent service. Price would be secondary. With this sort of experience, what do you think the customer will remember most? The price of meat or the personal service they received? I'll bet on the service. Do you get this kind of service at the grocery store where you spend your hard-earned money? Why not?

I recently experienced the best service ever at a grocery store. I got in line where the checker greeted me, she rang me up promptly, bagged my groceries appropriately, and thanked me for coming in. Who was my checker? Me. I did the self checkout.

Has it come to that? What exceptional service do you provide to your customer?

Rewind...to Training the Customer

Now that I've thought about it, I may have to change my answer—slightly—the next time someone asks if it's possible to train the customer. Actually...in a way...it is. A colleague of mine worked for many years in the hospitality industry, most recently at a private membership club that prided itself on catering to its members. At one Monday morning staff meeting, the primary subject was the recent training program for the new restaurant and banquet servers. Someone humorously made the remark, "Now if we could only train the *members*." The twelve employees seated around the conference table were shocked when the CEO quietly said, "but you *have* to." What? Train the members? Train the customers? Not as difficult as you might think. But then again, since it's not an active training session, the results aren't always as predictable or effective.

In simplest terms, you have to *help* create good customers. If your policies and services are clearly understood; if their questions and concerns are answered; if mottos are lived up to; if staff is attentive, focused, and *in the moment,* you have trained the customer for what to expect. The responsibility still lies with you. And the better you do your job, the better you have trained your customer.

Customer Appreciation Day / Week

What does that mean? It means that every single day we appreciate our customers but during this particular day/week, we are going to put the full-force focus there. Some suggestions for hosting an event like this:

> ➢ Invite both current and potential customers. Remember, the current customers are happy; and if you invite potential customers, the current customers become your additional marketing staff.
> ➢ Provide a sign-in book and follow up with a short handwritten note thanking all who attend.

- ➢ Involve your staff in networking, serving food, handing out goodies, etc. Provide some tips to staff for networking (not everyone automatically knows how to do this). Practice introductions, handshakes, etc.
- ➢ Involve all management staff, Board of Directors, investors, vendors, etc.
- ➢ Serve food and refreshments.
- ➢ Advertise all of the items that will be available that day.
- ➢ Provide promotional items to all who attend.
- ➢ Focus on the children by providing bouncing blow ups, balloons, clowns, candy, etc.
- ➢ Take pictures of the event and submit to the local media. Also include in your company's newsletters.

How do you appreciate your customer?

"Pretend that every single person you meet has a sign around his or her neck that says, Make Me Feel Important. Not only will you succeed in sales, you will succeed in life."
~ Mary Kay Ash ~

Customer Appreciation Moment

Sometimes it doesn't require a week, or even a day. Sometimes a moment is all it takes to be a mini-hero in your customers' eyes. A mutual client (we patronize each other's businesses) had been having what was beginning to feel like a continual run of equipment problems. Just when one thing was repaired, it seemed another one would break down. It ran the gamut from minor to major and in between, and, understandably, her frustration was winning the war.

During the most recent equipment breakdown, she was having problems locating the part necessary for repair; and when she finally did, it was only sold by a company that was nearly an hour's drive from her location. Business commitments made it nearly impossible for her to make the trip to pick up the part, which she explained to the company rep. He understood the situation and sympathized with it—and offered to UPS it to her at a surprisingly affordable rate, promising that it would be there in a day's time.

She was happy enough when the small package arrived the next day. But when she reached inside the box, her face lit up like a kid on Christmas morning. "They sent me a Blowpop!" she said, laughing and holding it up for the staff to see. Not only was it a light-hearted and unexpected surprise, but they had chosen the flavor perfectly to match her logo colors. And that was all it took. Small wow, big impact.

What is your lollipop?

Being the Customer

I am the first person to say that everyone deserves good customer service. I am also the first to say that the customer has a responsibility to make that happen.

Here is an example: I was volunteering at a homecoming and I was working the cash register at a fish booth. The line was long, but thanks to the quick efforts of the volunteers the line was moving quite quickly. Things are going along smoothly and I'm ready to help the next person in line. I said, "Hello, what can I get you today?" She just stared at me—while she was on the telephone. So, thinking she was busy, I went on to the next person—with the full intent to serve the person on the telephone as soon as she had finished her call.

As I began to assist Customer B, Customer A said to her caller, "Hold on." Then she looked at me and said, "Hey! I was next!" I said, "I'm sorry. I thought you would want to finish your conversation and then order." She said, "I am in line, and it doesn't matter if I am on the phone or not. I am next."

"Okay," I said to her, "can I take your order?" Then she said to the person on the telephone, "What do you want? Chicken or fish?" Unbelievable.

I have another telephone story. One of the local fast food restaurants posts a sign that says, "Please do not use your cell phone when you are in the drive through line." The first time I saw the sign I thought to myself, "Who do they think they are telling me when I can use my phone?" But then I remembered the homecoming incident, and I could understand what they were saying. In talking with many people in the service industry, this may very well be the biggest pet peeve of all.

Other pet peeves – when the customer, for some reason, believes they are better than the person assisting them. While I was in college I worked full time, went to school full time. and worked part time at a bowling alley. The money for me was just a little extra spending money. One night I was in a rather happy mood, and one of the customers asked me why I was so cheerful. I explained to them that on Saturday I would graduate with my Master's Degree. He sort of laughed and said, "You go to college? What kind of degree would YOU be getting?" I explained that I would receive a dual Master's Degree in Management and Human Resource Development. His reply was, "I just didn't even think you were smart. You're just a waitress." I was really hurt. And his rudeness shocked me. He had no idea *who* or *what* I was. Just because you have a certain job does not mean that you are stupid or incompetent. Please, don't ever assume.

It goes the other way as well. Just because you see someone in a business suit, don't always assume they are smart. Instead of assuming, (and making a fool of yourself) how about getting to know them? You just never know. After frequenting a restaurant, I learned that the waitress worked on the weekends to pay for college. She had been going for fifteen years and working in the restaurant all that time so that she could come out of college debt free. I would constantly see people look down on her, and I never understood why. My reaction was *more power to her!*

Notes

Chapter Sixteen

Happy Endings

Holiday Shoppers

Ah, the holidays. It's a beautiful and insanely hectic time. Everyone is busy shopping, finding that perfect gift...and instead of visions of sugarplums dancing, it's more like a whirl-wind—thoughts of baking, wrapping, holiday cards, parties, out-of-town guests...there's just no end to the list. So if you're the retailer, the company, start gearing up early. Time will be as short as tempers, and customer service heroes will be your best commodity.

Officially the season kicks off on Black Friday, the day after Thanksgiving wearing the crown as the busiest shopping day of the year. I know some people who refuse to even leave their house on that day, not wanting to fight the crowds and the traffic. But what this season means to the retailer, and the purpose it serves, is to act as a primary indicator of the upcoming year—providing, of course, a huge percentage of current year revenue, but also predicting the shape of things to come.

So, that being said, it seems like the perfect time for the retailers to put their best foot forward. But, do they really do that? Remember, many shoppers utilize different types of stores when looking for specialized gifts. Many are there for the first time, acquiring that all-important first impression. If it isn't a good one, you might as well also predict that they won't be back in the new year.

It is the ideal time to step up customer service (although it should be great all year round) and let your staff know that the sales now really do affect next year's sales. So, what can you do? Here are some suggestions:

➢ Offer greeters at the door (or position someone there, maybe filling shelves) to welcome customers, thank them when they leave, and assist them in finding a particular item.

➢ Acquire the customer's mailing or email address so that you may add them to your database, to be used during sales, etc.

➢ Give them a small gift—a small token of thanks.

➢ Consider implementing additional self-service options to eliminate long lines: price-scanning, gift location, gift cards, etc.

➢ Pay special attention to the cleanliness of your business.

➢ Remind your staff of the importance of upselling.

➢ Encourage staff to introduce themselves to all customers, to begin to build relationships.

➢ Extend holiday hours as needed.

➢ Bring on extra staff as needed (but be sure that they are thoroughly trained).

Use the hectic holiday shopping season to your best advantage. Knowing that it's going to be a difficult one for your customer service reps, it would be the perfect time to think of some incentives for them as well. If you treat your employees the way you and *they* should treat the customers, it just might be contagious. Customer satisfaction is difficult without employee satisfaction.

The Complaint Department

*"Your most unhappy customers
are your greatest source of learning."*
~ Bill Gates ~

As much as you try, you can never satisfy every single customer. Everyone has different expectations, some attainable for you and some not. In certain instances, you will encounter customers who are simply not a good fit for your company. So how do you handle those customers who have complaints? Here are some suggestions:

➢ Act quickly, stay polite and professional.
➢ Listen to their complaint and let them explain the situation. Be open with your body language—no folded arms allowed. It makes you look defensive.
➢ If you notice they are becoming loud, it is best to remove them from the situation. Many customers complain and wish to draw an audience. You do not need to have an audience.

- ➢ After the customer voices their complaint, summarize to them what you heard. That will show them that you were listening.
- ➢ Ask the customer what they believe it would take to resolve the situations. Sometimes you will find that it is an easy solution and sometimes you will find that it is an unreasonable request. At least you have a starting point.
- ➢ Come up with what you believe is a fair plan, asking the customer if they believe it is a fair plan.
- ➢ Put the plan in writing (if necessary).
- ➢ Thank the person for bringing the complaint to your attention.
- ➢ Follow up with a handwritten note.
- ➢ If employees were involved within the complaint, meet with them individually to discuss.

In some cases, complaints cannot be resolved. There may be times that customers just need to separate from your business. Although this should be very rare, it does happen.

I have seen complaints handled so well that the customer walked away thanking the business. I have seen complaints handled so poorly that I wondered how the manager got the position that he did.

Help your staff work through complaints by role playing with them, letting them be the customer. Seeing it done properly and improperly will be of huge assistance for them. Also, remember that they are watching you as their manager and how you react.

"The first responsibility of a leader is to define reality.The last is to say thank you. In between, the leader is a servant."
~ Max DePree ~

Looking Back

I have a friend who demands excellent service. At some level, there is nothing wrong with that. One day I happened to stop by her office to go to lunch. She had a client waiting for her who had arrived before I did, so I waited as she came out to greet the client. I was amazed—actually appalled—at the way she greeted her. There was no handshake. There was no eye contact. There was no thank you at the end. In fact, when we got in the car, she did nothing but complain about that client (something that you should never do). I said to her, "I understand that you expect excellent service, but I have to say that I don't believe you are *giving* it." She was totally taken aback. She couldn't see it. I asked her to do a couple things the next time she saw a client—the handshake, the eye contact. She was amazed that she was previously giving service that she would not tolerate herself.

⚜

Sometimes it's important to just step back and look at how you do things. Some days I am my own best example. Even though I teach it, work it, and have written about it, I can say that I'm not always on my "A" game. If I could create the shortest customer service cheat sheet known to man, it might say, "Nip it, walk it, be it, just do it." But...what I always have to remember is that the person in my office *right now* deserves the same time and respect as anyone else...as *everyone* else.

It doesn't matter if "right now" is six o'clock. It doesn't matter if I have had a rough day. It doesn't matter if I have dealt with nothing but problems all day, I feel like I've been hit by a bus, and I just want to go home. It is not their problem. I should stand up and greet them with a handshake, always have a smile, and offer to help them in any way I can. At that moment, they are the most important person in my life.

Notes

About the Author

Customer Service and Beyond joined the corporate crowd in 2001, a company developed to assist businesses of any size with customer service training ... *and beyond*. Then, as now, it was the goal of CEO Dawn Mushill to remind every tread on the corporate stair that it's all about the WOW! And how to get it back if they'd lost it. Now she brings us that same message and reminder in her first book.

A native of Granite City, Illinois, Dawn Johnson and her husband Ted currently reside in nearby Troy, sharing their busy lives with three cats and a very-outnumbered dog. For the past eight years she has served as Executive Director of the Troy/Maryville Area Chamber of Commerce; and in that period she has gathered a lifetime's measure of community involvement and customer service.

With more than fifteen years of training experience in various venues, Dawn's academic background comprises an Associate's Degree in Secretarial Science; a Bachelor's Degree in Education, Training and Development; and a dual Master's

Degree in Management and Human Resource Development. She has trained for more than 200 companies and conducted presentations for thousands of people. And knowing Dawn, she's probably remembered most of their names.

In 2004 she was awarded the "Key to the City" from Troy, Illinois Mayor Tom Caraker; and in subsequent years was recognized and honored with the *2005 Career Mentor of the Year* and the *2008 Distinguished Alumnus Award* from Southwestern Illinois College.

Every speaking engagement is a new highlight for Dawn, but some of the larger moments include serving as keynote speaker for the 2005 Illinois Phi Beta Lambda State Conference; the 2005 Illinois Business and Professional Women's State Conference; both the 2006 and 2008 Growth Association Women's Conferences; the 2007 and 2008 Illinois Federation of Teachers' Conferences in Chicago; and the 2008 Working Women's Survival Show in St. Charles, Missouri.

Dawn walks the talk—and she does it with passion—customizing each training session and developing programs with an exclusive focus on the individual customer. She guarantees and continually offers a fun and lively environment for learning. Her training presentations and keynote speaking events are engaging, energetic, and enthusiastic, lending humor and anecdotal color to the very serious business of customer service.

Quote sources:

www.thinkexist.com

www.brainyquotes.com

www.wisdomquotes.com

www.woopidoo.com

www.worldofquotes.com

Bring Dawn to Your Company
to Teach the WOW Factor

CEO Dawn Mushill creates corporate training programs with an exclusive focus on the individual customer, dissecting problem areas and behavior while she guides and educates.

But if you're expecting a dry and bland seminar you'll be delightfully surprised!

Dawn's training presentations are the polar opposite, as she offers an engaging and enthusiastic environment for learning...for succeeding.

The atmosphere is an innovative mix—entertaining and educational—as she blends humor and professionalism to lend her own comfortable take on the incredibly serious business of customer service.

Let *Customer Service and Beyond* bring the **WOW** factor back to your business—whether packaged as a fundamental refresher course or start-from-scratch training. Developed in detail and derived from her findings through secret shopping and onsite evaluations, Dawn provides the essential tools to build a thriving and dynamic company.

Astonish your customers, exceed their expectations, boost employee morale...it's all possible with a customized training session designed specifically for you and your staff. Who would have ever guessed that success could be so fun...

For further details and contact information, please visit www.customerserviceandbeyond.com.

FOR ADDITIONAL COPIES OF THIS BOOK

PLEASE COMPLETE THE FORM BELOW AND MAIL TO:
Customer Service and Beyond ~ PO Box 314 ~ Troy, IL 62294

Please print:

Name/Title: _____

Company: _____

Address: _____

City: _____ State: _____ Zip: _____

E-mail address: _____

Payment Method: Enclose check or money order (allow 2 weeks for processing) or pay via credit card / PayPal according to the guidelines below.

____ Check (payable to Customer Service and Beyond)

____ Money Order (payable to Customer Service and Beyond)

____ Credit Card (visit www.customerserviceandbeyond.com)

____ Number of copies ($19.95 + $2.00 shipping fee for each book)

All orders will receive a complimentary bookmark -- just our way of saying *thank you*. If you would like an autographed copy, please let us know to whom you would like it inscribed.

Thank you for your order. We'd love to know how you heard about us:

_____

_____

_____

_____

Printed in the United States
216227BV00002B/1/P